LEOPOLDSTADT

Also by Tom Stoppard

TOM STOPPARD

LEOPOLDSTADT

Grove Press
New York

First published in 2020 in Great Britain by Faber and Faber Limited, London.

Printed in the United States of America

ISBN 978-0-8021-5771-3
eISBN 978-0-8021-5772-0

Grove Press
an imprint of Grove Atlantic
154 West 14th Street
New York, NY 10011

Distributed by Publishers Group West

groveatlantic.com

23   10 9 8 7

For Sabrina

Author's Note

Patrick Marber was my first reader at every stage.
His notes had a beneficial effect on *Leopoldstadt* from first to last.

The staff at the London Library were helpful as ever. Among the books I profited from are *Emancipation* by Michael Goldfarb, *The Hare with Amber Eyes* by Edmund de Waal, *The House of Wittgenstein* by Alexander Waugh, *Last Waltz in Vienna* by George Clare, and *Jews, Anti-Semitism and Culture in Vienna*, an indispensable collection of essays by various hands (ed. Ivar Oxaal et al.). Steven Beller's *A Concise History of Austria* was my backcloth.

Alistair Summers helped me with the Seder and the *bris milah*, and Daniel Kehlmann patiently answered many questions about matters Austrian and Viennese.

My thanks go to all of the above, and to Sonia Friedman, begetter and producer, whose commitment has been unconditional.

Simon Trussler (1942–2019) was my copyeditor for my most recent plays. We spent many gentle ruminative hours on the phone preparing texts for the printer. We never met. Simon died after completing the first proof copy of *Leopoldstadt*.

PRODUCTION CREDITS

Leopoldstadt was produced by Sonia Friedman Productions and was first performed at Wyndham's Theatre, London, on 25 January 2020.

The cast was as follows:

Wilma	Clara Francis
Grandma Emilia	Caroline Gruber
Hermann	Adrian Scarborough
Eva	Alexis Zegerman
Gretl	Faye Castelow
Ernst	Aaron Neil
Young Sally	Maya Larholm / Libby Lewis / Beatrice Rapstone
Jana	Natalie Law
Young Rosa	Olivia Festinger / Tamar Laniado / Chloe Raphael
Young Jacob	Jarlan Bogolubov / Daniel Lawson / Ramsay Robertson
Ludwig	Ed Stoppard
Pauli	Ilan Galkoff
Hanna	Dorothea Myer-Bennett
Hilde	Felicity Davidson
Poldi	Sadie Shimmin
Fritz	Luke Thallon

Hermine	Yasmin Paige
Jacob	Sebastian Armesto
Nellie	Eleanor Wyld
Rosa	Jenna Augen
Kurt	Alexander Newland
Aaron	Griffin Stevens
Zac	Joe Coen
Sally	Avye Leventis
Otto	Noof McEwan
Mohel	Jake Neads
Young Nathan	Rhys Bailey
Percy	Sam Hoare
Young Leo	Toby Cohen / Jack Meredith / Joshua Schneider
Bella	Olivia Festinger / Tamar Laniado / Chloe Raphael
Mimi	Maya Larholm / Libby Lewis / Beatrice Rapstone
Civilian	Mark Edel-Hunt
Policeman	Joe Coen
Policeman	Jake Neads
Heini	Zachary Cohen / Louis Levy / Montague Rapstone
Nathan	Sebastian Armesto
Leo	Luke Thallon
Director	Patrick Marber
Set Designer	Richard Hudson
Costume Designer	Brigitte Reiffenstuel

Lighting Designer	Neil Austin
Sound Designer & Original Music	Adam Cork
Movement	E J Boyle
Casting	Amy Ball CDG
Children's Casting	Verity Naughton

The production, with the same creativeteam, subsequently opened at the Longacre Theatre in New York on 2 October 2022.

The cast was as follows:

Wilma	Jenna Augen
Grandma Emilia	Betsy Aidem
Hermann	David Krumholtz
Eva	Caissie Levy
Gretl	Faye Castelow
Ernst	Aaron Neil
Young Sally	Reese Bogin / Romy Fay
Jana	Sara Topham
Young Rosa	Pearl Scarlett Gold / Ava Michele Hyl
Young Jacob	Joshua Satine / Aaron Shuf
Ludwig	Brandon Uranowitz
Pauli	Drew Squire
Hanna	Colleen Litchfield
Hilde	Eden Epstein
Poldi	Gina Ferrall

Fritz	Arty Froushan
Hermine	Eden Epstein
Jacob	Seth Numrich
Nellie	Tedra Millan
Rosa	Jenna Augen
Kurt	Daniel Cantor
Aaron	Jesse Aaronson
Zac	Matt Harrington
Sally	Sara Topham
Otto	Japhet Balaban
Mohel	Daniel Cantor
Young Nathan	Anthony Rosenthal
Percy	Seth Numrich
Young Leo	Michael Deaner / Wesley Holloway
Bella	Pearl Scarlett Gold / Ava Michele Hyl
Mimi	Reese Bogin / Romy Fay
Civilian	Corey Brill
Policeman	Jesse Aaronson
Policeman	Matt Harrington
Heini	Max Ryan Burach / Calvin James Davis / Jaxon Cain Grundleger
Nathan	Brandon Uranowitz
Leo	Arty Froushan

CHARACTERS

Grandma Emilia

Hermann, her son

Eva, her daughter

Gretl, married to Hermann

Ludwig, married to Eva

Wilma, sister of Ludwig

Ernst, married to Wilma

Hanna, sister of Ludwig and Wilma

Jacob, son of Hermann and Gretl

Pauli, son of Ludwig and Eva

Nellie, daughter of Ludwig and Eva

Sally, daughter of Ernst and Wilma

Rosa, Sally's twin

Poldi, cook/housekeeper

Hilde, parlour maid

Jana, nursemaid

Fritz, a young officer

Hermine, daughter of Hanna and Kurt

Aaron, married to Nellie

Kurt, married to Hanna

Zac, married to Sally

Otto, a banker

Mohel

Percy, an English journalist

Leo, son of Nellie and Aaron

Nathan, son of Sally and Zac

Mimi, daughter of Sally and Zac

Bella, Mimi's twin

Heini, son of Hermine and Otto

Civilian

SCENE ONE

Vienna, December 1899.

At the prosperous end of Viennese bourgeoisie, twelve members of two intermarried Jewish families, and a housekeeper-cook (POLDI), a parlour maid (HILDE) and a nursemaid (JANA), are variously occupied among the overcrowded, fussy furnishings of an apartment off the Ringstrasse.

The combined families are eight grown-ups and four children, plus an infant in a bassinet (NELLIE).

The apartment, spread over one floor of a grand high-ceilinged block, is the home of the Merz family, the occupancy now reduced to the matriarch, EMILIA Merz, her son HERMANN and his wife GRETL, and their son JACOB, who is eight.

Two familial groups are the visitors: Hermann's sister EVA with her husband LUDWIG, and their two children, PAULI, aged eight, and the baby, NELLIE. WILMA is Ludwig's sister, married to ERNST. They have two daughters, SALLY and ROSA, who are twins and younger than Jacob. Finally there is Wilma's unmarried sister HANNA who is eighteen.

Gretl is gentile. So is Ernst.

Poldi, aged about forty, and Hilde are in the Merz household. Jana has come with the baby but is supervising the children.

The grown-ups have been served coffee in dainty cups.

Several balls are in the air from the word go, and little or no sense can be made except that chocolate cake with whipped cream is going round on little plates delivered by Poldi and Hilde, and a Christmas tree is being decorated by the four children, overseen by Jana.

Emilia is at a table dispensing the chocolate cake, cutting slices and adding a large dollop of whipped cream to each plate. For this purpose she has put aside the family photo album.

Hermann, solo, is fulminating over a thin 'book', a pamphlet of 80 pages.

Eva is confiding scandal to Gretl over another small book.

Ernst is talking to Ludwig about a third book.

Wilma is seated where she can talk to Emilia or intervene in any squabbles between the children. She is turning the pages of the photo album.

Hanna is playing the piano for herself. She is playing 'Stille Nacht! Heil'ge Nacht!'

The Christmas decorations come from a large box: silver balls, bells, streamers, paper chains, stale iced biscuits and chocolates shaped like little animals, soldiers, musical instruments etc.

Thus the chatter of the children finds room where it may over, under and between Emilia's instructions to Poldi, the proffering of cake and the receiving of cake, and such tête-à-tête conversation as can be made out between the sisters-in-law (Eva and Gretl) and between the brothers-in-law (Ernst and Ludwig), all to the sound of 'Stille Nacht!' on the piano.

CHILDREN . . . That's mine. He took my silver bell, Jana! . . . Don't pull on the paper chain, Sally, you'll break it . . . It needs more over here . . . The snowflakes have to go on last . . . This one's broken . . . I need a hook for the reindeer . . . Rosa, you can do the snow round the tree, there's cotton wool for that . . . The little trumpet works, toot-toot! . . . (*Etc.*)

WILMA (*showing a photo*) Who's this, Emilia?

EMILIA Hermann's father, when we were engaged.

Hermann throws his pamphlet down with an angry snort.

HERMANN Imbecile!

Seeing that everybody is occupied, he picks it up again and resumes reading.

EVA (*to Gretl*)   . . . like a daisy chain, two by two . . . 'Hello'—drops her drawers—'Bye-bye'—'Next!'—'Hello'—drops her drawers—'Bye-bye'—'Next!'—

Gretl covers her mouth at the audacity of it.

GRETL   Eva!

EVA   —changing partners, like a round dance.

ERNST (*to Ludwig*)   . . . Interpreting dreams, you will recall, got Joseph out of prison in Egypt and into a top job with the Pharaoh . . . but the Viennese medical fraternity is more conservative, even though half of them would still be in the land of Canaan . . .

SALLY (*straying*)   Can I have mine, Grannie Emilia?

EMILIA   You can when you finish the tree. We only have a tree for you little Papists.

WILMA   Ernst is Protestant, Emilia.

EMILIA   It's still a nice Jewish boy with ideas about himself—you can hit a dozen like him throwing chestnuts across the Danube Canal.

Sally returns to the tree.

GRETL (*to Eva*)   Well, can I be after you with it?

JANA   You're not allowed to eat the decorations, Rosa. I saw you, Missy.

ROSA   I only licked it.

JACOB   I've got the star for the top, Mummy! I want to do it, Jana.

JANA   Hold on to me, then.

Jacob has to stand on a chair to reach the top of the tree.
Hermann throws his pamphlet aside again.

LUDWIG (*to Ernst*)   Hysteria, neurosis . . . the more modern the diagnosis, the more the treatment returns to its origins in the priesthood. So, yes, the interpretation of dreams, why not?

ERNST   But he has no connections and no followers. He should have been *extraordinarius* by now.

Hermann has come over and hovered.

HERMANN (*to Ernst*)   He should go to Argentina. He'd be a professor in no time.

ERNST   Why Argentina?

HERMANN   Or Africa. Palestine is a lost cause so long as it's ruled by the Ottomans. Or Madagascar! They say there's plenty of room for a Jewish state in Madagascar.

LUDWIG   Madagascar with Jews—it sounds a bit like a dream in itself.

HERMANN (*dismissively*)   A pipe dream.

GRETL (*with Eva's book*)   Inscribed to Ludwig . . . !

EVA   Arthur couldn't get it published, let alone put on, so he printed a few copies for his friends. Ask Hermann.

JACOB   Look, Mummy!

GRETL (*not looking*)   That's lovely, darling. (*To Eva.*) Hermann's in a temper about having his own country somewhere.

EVA   I'll leave it here for you.

JACOB   You're not looking!

Gretl and Eva turn to look. Jacob's star at the top of the tree is a large golden Star of David.

EVA (*momentarily bewildered*)   Is that right?

EMILIA (*looking*)   Oy.

GRETL   It's a beautiful star, darling, but it's not the star we put at the top of our Christmas tree.

PAULI   I'll find it. I know which one it is.

JACOB   What's wrong with it?

EMILIA   Poor boy, baptised and circumcised in the same week, what can you expect?

Jacob accepts the right star from Pauli.

GRETL   It's true. He yelled both times.

EVA   I don't understand my brother—he got himself Christianised long before he met you, Gretl, and married you in church like a good Catholic, so why . . . ?

GRETL   He's just a man, he doesn't want his son to be different from him.

Eva laughs. Hermann is instinctively drawn to investigate.

HERMANN   What are you talking about?

EMILIA   Foreskins. Hanna, can't you play something else?

Hanna stops playing. Ludwig and Ernst pay some attention.

EVA   With my Pauli it's simple. We're Jews. Bad Jews but pure-blood sons of Abraham, and Ludwig's parents would have nothing to do with us if their grandson didn't look Jewish in his bath. In fact, if I'd had myself Christianised like Hermann, Ludwig wouldn't have married me, would you, be honest.

LUDWIG   I would when they were dead.

EVA   Is that a compliment?

LUDWIG (*mildly*)   Honour thy father and thy mother. (*Noting Wilma's reaction.*) I didn't mean that the way it sounded. (*Bowing his head to Ernst.*) And Ernst. Of course. Mathematics is the only language in which you can make yourself clear, I find. You really ought to come to Momma and Poppa for Seder this year, Wilma, with Ernst and the girls, naturally.

WILMA   I should. It might be her last year.

LUDWIG (*to Hermann*)   You and Gretl too, of course. It would be nice for the cousins to do Seder together.

GRETL   I'll come. What happens at Seder?

HERMANN (*to Ludwig*)   You seem to think becoming a Catholic is like joining the Jockey Club.

LUDWIG   It's not unlike, except that anyone can become a Catholic.

WILMA   You're snobby about Grannie and Grandpa Jakobovicz, Hermann, if I may say so.

HERMANN   I?

WILMA   Yes, you. You're snobby about their accent and using Yiddish words, and dressing like immigrants from some village in Galicia except they're still there, keeping the village shop, there's too much of the shtetl about them for you.

HERMANN   That's not being snobby, it's being . . . no, snobby, yes, I admit it.

GRETL   I'd like to see Galicia, Hermann. It will be interesting.

HERMANN   How can it be interesting?

EVA (*peacemaking*)   For that matter, everyone can come to us for Seder, can't they, Ludwig?

HANNA   Oh, yes please, Eva!

WILMA (*to Hanna*)   What about Momma and Poppa?

EVA   Them too. Vienna will be exciting for them. It's only changing trains.

WILMA   Changing what train? It takes half a day to *get* to the train, and she'll want to bring her bedding, not to mention enough food to open a restaurant. She'll spend three weeks getting ready, getting more nervous every day and worrying about leaving the shop . . . In fact, with her heart it will probably kill her.

LUDWIG   There's nothing wrong with her heart, but even so . . .

WILMA   Who are you to say that?

LUDWIG   Who is Doctor Lissak to say it, do you mean? Even so . . .

WILMA   Just like a son! Momma and Poppa denied themselves everything so they could be proud of you getting into the university—

LUDWIG   I was agreeing with you.

Hanna from her place at the piano bursts out.

HANNA   What about me? When is anybody going to be proud of me getting out into anywhere? It's all very well for you, Wilma, you never gave Momma a thought when you snapped up your brother's university friend regardless whether he was a Jew or a Hottentot! I want to come to Vienna for Passover!

Gretl goes to her to comfort her.

GRETL   And so you shall, won't she, Hermann? When's Passover?

HERMANN (*shrugs*)   How do I know . . . March, April . . . but anyway we're likely to be in the Italian Lakes again next—

WILMA   No! (*To Gretl.*) Stop interfering. We're going to Momma and Poppa. It might be her last chance to show she's forgiven me for marrying Ernst.

EMILIA   If she hasn't, you can bring the girls to me, Wilma. Unless it's the same time as Easter. I don't mind Christmas because baby Jesus had no idea what was going on, but I feel funny about Easter eggs.

HERMANN (*to Ernst*)   You seem to have been struck dumb.

13

ERNST Who wouldn't be?

GRETL I have to go anyway, I've got a sitting.

JACOB What's a sitting? Can I come?

GRETL No, darling, I can't be changing my expression while you're fidgeting.

Hanna speaks to Gretl while life goes on.

During the conversation between Gretl and Hanna, the Christmas tree is completed, admiration is expressed. Eva and Wilma have brought wrapped Christmas presents, for the Merz family, to be put under the tree now. Naturally Jacob is inquisitive prematurely ('Which is mine?') and is rebuffed ('Wait and see!') and the twins are made excitable by identifying the presents they themselves have brought for Jacob. There is a total of about a dozen parcels, including Pauli's presents to the Merz family, which Pauli 'announces' as he places them under the tree. Eva and Wilma get the children under control and assemble them around Emilia's table to be given chocolate cake.

The men—Hermann, Ludwig and Ernst—take a token part in all this while having their cups replenished by Hilde, supplied with a fresh pot by Poldi. The baby wakes up. Jana quietens her.

None of this obscures the words exchanged by Gretl and Hanna.

HANNA Gretl, can I tell you something? I've met someone.

GRETL (*pleased*) Oh, Hanna! Tell me at once.

HANNA He's an officer in the Dragoons, and he—he likes me.

GRETL Of course he does! A Dragoon! Yellow or Black?

HANNA I don't know, he wasn't in uniform.

GRETL Where were you introduced?

HANNA We weren't exactly . . .

GRETL How did you meet him?

HANNA He just spoke to me in the street.

GRETL Oh.

HANNA He and his friend. They were very polite. They saw me getting off the tram at the corner of the Opera.

GRETL And then what?

HANNA They said, can they have the honour of taking me for tea at the Imperial. They were so amusing. Then the other one had to leave.

GRETL The other one?

HANNA Yes. Theodor. Fritz, the one I liked, asked me to dance. Oh, Gretl, you should have seen me!—whirled around in the arms of a dashing young officer with the violins and squeeze-boxes going mad till I could have fainted!—Miss Hanna Jakobovicz in society! Then I had to go because I always help to put the girls to bed when I stay with Wilma and Ernst. Fritz asked if he could walk me home, and I said he'd have to walk me to Galicia but I'm sure Mummy and Daddy would ask him in—I know, I could die when I think of me gabbling non-stop and making silly jokes, but he said he'll walk me to my sister's this time but we should have tea again before I go home, and he invited me to tea at his place tomorrow.

GRETL Goodness. Did you say yes?

HANNA No. I said no, the very idea! I don't want Fritz to think I'm that kind of girl. So I said—not unless I could bring a friend. So, will you?

GRETL Me?

HANNA I haven't got any friends in Vienna, and you're like a friend. Will you?

GRETL Oh, Hanna . . .

HANNA Please will you? Or I won't go.

GRETL Well . . . why not? Of course I will.

Hanna embraces her. They remain together laughing together.
Hanna starts playing a waltz.
Ernst and Ludwig have ended up resuming their conversation.

ERNST (*to Ludwig*) . . . There's something about a theory being published at the very beginning of a new century. Like an augury. Like the curtain going up on something.

LUDWIG New centuries just depend on when you start counting. But I don't doubt that dreams can tell us something about ourselves. I sometimes dream I've proved the Riemann Hypothesis. In fact—

He calls to Eva.

Eva! Would you like to go to Paris this summer for the Exposition?

GRETL (*returning from Hanna*) I'll come!

EVA Paris? What's going on? I can't get you to come to Ischl for a few days in the country, and now—

GRETL Of course you must.

ERNST Vienna will be there in force. Mahler is taking the Philharmonic to the Paris Exposition.

LUDWIG There you are.

ERNST He's taking his Second Symphony to annoy the French.

EVA We went to the premiere of the Second Symphony, Ludwig, and you didn't like it.

LUDWIG That's not the point. He's our man.

EMILIA Another Christian still wet from his baptism.

LUDWIG And we're sending the 'Philosophy' painting for the university to show the Parisians. I was asked to sign a petition got up against it by the philosophy faculty.

GRETL Did you hear that, Hermann? My painter is going to be exhibited at the World's Fair in Paris!

LUDWIG   The faculty wants Plato and Aristotle discussing ideas in an olive grove, they don't want modern art stuck up on the ceiling of the University and calling itself 'Philosophy'. We can have a look at it in Paris.

EVA   Ludwig, you couldn't be bothered to cross the road—

LUDWIG   I would have done if I wasn't so busy, but at the World Exposition the honour of Vienna is at stake, in art, in music, and to give Paris its due, you might buy one or two dresses, say two at the most—

GRETL   Eva! You have to go.

EVA (*suspiciously*)   And what will you be doing?

LUDWIG   As it happens, the Second International Conference of Mathematicians is to be held in Paris during the Exposition, which will give me the opportunity to meet some mathematicians I'm in correspondence with.

EVA   Well, if you're going with or without me, I'm coming.

GRETL (*wheedling*)   Oh, Hermann! I want to go to the mathematical conference!

ERNST   Will Riemann be there?

LUDWIG   Riemann is dead.

ERNST   What about his wife?—No, that was in bad taste—

The baby starts crying.

GRETL   I'm late. I have to take my green shawl . . . !

There follows a confusion of moves and utterances.
  Hermann picks up Gretl's green shawl.
  Pauli jogs the bassinet with a concerned interest in the baby.

PAULI   It's all right, Nellie, don't cry. Open your eyes, look, it's me, your brother Pauli.

Hermann brings the shawl to Gretl and drapes it tenderly around her.

HERMANN   Look at you! *He* should be paying *me*!

GRETL   No, no—then how would I know my portrait is because you love me?

HERMANN   It is!

GRETL   Kiss me, then, on the mouth, nobody's looking.

HERMANN   Yes, they are.

Gretl laughs, then ambushes him with a fleeting kiss on the lips, and hurries out. Hermann is pleased.

During the above Eva picks up Nellie, quietening her with endearments. Hilde is tidying up the coffee things to remove them on a tray: she is politely thanked here and there. The children meanwhile are in a back-and-forth with Emilia—see below. Then Ernst, at Wilma's suggestion, is rounding up children. Hanna has continued to play Strauss.

EVA (*to Nellie*)   There, there, who didn't get their chocolate cake? (*To Jana.*) I'll give her a feed. The children are going to get some fresh air and see the camels in Stephansplatz. Make sure Pauli has his gloves—

LUDWIG   Camels?

EVA   The Nativity scene.

EMILIA   Who wants to lick the spoon?

CHILDREN   I will . . . Me, me . . . Yes please, Grandma Emilia . . . I'm the oldest, Grandma . . .

EMILIA   The first one to say 'You have it, Grandma' would have got the cream, but no one said it, so—

She licks the cream spoon.

WILMA   Thank you, Hanna! All hands on deck. Coats on, coats on!

Hanna abandons the piano and goes out.

HERMANN   Jacob, have you told Uncle Ludwig?

LUDWIG   Told me what?

HERMANN   Come, Jacob . . . tell your uncle.

JACOB   I was first in my class for mathematics.

LUDWIG   My word. Well done!

HERMANN   His teacher says he's a natural.

LUDWIG   I congratulate you, Jacob. You have great pleasures in store. Numbers are a huge toy box, we can play with them and make amazing, beautiful things.

HERMANN   Ask him something!

LUDWIG   What are you hoping to get for Christmas?

HERMANN   I mean, test him, you'll see.

LUDWIG   Oh, well . . . do you think you can add together all the numbers between one and ten in your head?

HERMANN   That's too easy. Go on, Jacob. (*Generally.*) Not so much noise!

Jacob concentrates and calculates. Hermann watches expectantly.

WILMA   Are you going with them, Ernst?

ERNST   No, I've got to show up at the Neurology department.

WILMA   Did you have to have a patient *today*?

ERNST   No . . .

WILMA   You didn't do this last year.

ERNST   I wasn't *extraordinarius* last year. It's just one drink with the lecturers—and a 'Merry Christmas' to the assistants . . . it's expected.

JACOB   Fifty-five!

Ludwig pats him on the head. Hermann is pleased. Hanna has come in with woollen hats and scarves for the children.

LUDWIG Quite right. And fifty-five is five elevens. That's interesting.

HANNA Come on, Jacob!

Jacob runs to have his coat put on.

LUDWIG (*to Hermann*) About average.

HERMANN (*nettled*) What do you mean? Wasn't he right?

LUDWIG He answered correctly but he failed the test. Carl Friedrich Gauss when he was seven years old was asked to add all the numbers from one to a hundred. With barely a pause he answered 'Five thousand and fifty'. Now *that's* a natural.

HERMANN Was it the right answer?

LUDWIG Would I be telling you the story if it was not the right answer?

HERMANN A Jew might have made a guess, because there'd be a good chance the other person didn't know either.

Ludwig is amused.

LUDWIG But why a Jew?

HERMANN Don't you start. Is your Pauli a natural?

LUDWIG (*laughs*) He's obsessed with model soldiers. He can't wait to be in uniform.

One way or another, everyone except Emilia, Wilma, Hermann and Ludwig go on their way. Eva taking the baby out in her arms, and Poldi and Jana clearing the debris.
  Emilia settles down with the photo album.
  The brothers-in-law are not very close but they are comfortable with each other. Hermann offers Ludwig a cigar, but Ludwig prefers a cigarette. Hermann lights a cigar and pours two whiskies from a decanter.

HERMANN Well, what's the trick?

LUDWIG To see that you can add the numbers in any order you like . . . one plus ten, two plus nine, three plus eight . . . so each pair adds up to the same sum, for Jacob five elevens.

HERMANN He'll be better off being good at something useful. (*Faux pas.*) Something practical. In the circumstances. I don't mean mathematics isn't useful, of course.

LUDWIG Of course. Though number theory isn't. As far as we know.

HERMANN No doubt Eva has told you that Gretl can't have any more children, so all my money is on Jacob. An unfortunate expression, you're thinking.

LUDWIG Not at all. Admirably to the point.

HERMANN Best of all I would have liked my son to be a great composer. A virtuoso of the piano would be almost as good. But alas! So Jacob will take over Merz and Co from his father and grandfather as is the nature of things, and I'll have done my duty to the business.

Whisky in hand, they honour the moment with a silent toast, and settle themselves in chairs. There is a pause, which Emilia and Wilma fill.

EMILIA I've been writing in names that are missing, the ones I know, which is by no means all of them. That's what happens, you see. First, there's no need to write who they are, because everyone knows that's Great-Aunt Sophia or Cousin Rudi, and then only some of us know, and already we're asking, 'Who's that with Gertrude?' and 'I don't remember this man with the little dog', and you don't realise how fast they're disappearing from being remembered . . .

WILMA It's still an amazing thing to me, to know the faces of the dead! I can remember Grandpa Jakobovicz's tobacco-stained whiskers, but his wife died giving birth to Poppa before there were

21

photographs, so now no one knows what she looked like any more than if she'd been some kind of rumour.

EMILIA   Everyone was mad to have a photograph when I was a girl, it was like a miracle and you had to go to a photographer's to pose for him . . . wedding couples, soldiers in their first uniforms, children in front of painted scenery . . . and, always, women dressed up for the carnival ball, posing with a Greek pillar. Later, when we had a camera, there were too many pictures to keep in the album, holiday pictures with real scenery, swimming pictures, pictures of children in dirndl pinafores and lederhosen, like little Austrians. Here's a couple waving goodbye from the train, but who are they? No idea! That's why they're waving goodbye. It's like a second death, to lose your name in a family album.

She turns a page, writes a caption. She moves the album to Wilma and moves herself to a comfy chair where she soon dozes off. Wilma begins to stick loose photos into the album.
Meanwhile:

HERMANN   What do you think of the whisky? A gift from a supplier, best wool in Scotland, straight from the sheep. I happen to know our Emperor had it made up into a hunting jacket.

LUDWIG   Uh-hmm.

HERMANN   Did you say you have no use?

LUDWIG   In the sense that a composer has no use, compared to a textile manufacturer . . . yes. But pure mathematics is as absorbing as music. It's like finding the music in the untuned totality of number.

HERMANN   And do you get paid for that?

LUDWIG   Yes. I've no idea why. But if I went to sleep for a hundred years, the first thing I'd ask when I woke up is, 'Has Riemann been proved?'

HERMANN   Why?

LUDWIG   Because if it has, I can state with certainty how many prime numbers exist below a given number *however high*; and if it hasn't, I can't. Not with certainty.

HERMANN   That is a very annoying answer.

LUDWIG   Yes, but it has the saving grace that a number theorist, however great, is innocent of usefulness; unlike the applied mathematician who is the handmaiden of ballistics, modern architecture—

HERMANN   Are you great?

LUDWIG   No. But I have a student who might be, which is not nothing.

HERMANN   Is he a Jew?

LUDWIG   No.

HERMANN   He'll be a professor before you are.

LUDWIG   I hope so.

HERMANN   Oh, don't exaggerate! Why do Jews have to choose between pushy and humble? You're probably in line for the next Jew-slot. So don't fall for this Judenstaat idiocy. Do you want to do mathematics in the desert or in the city where Haydn, Mozart and Beethoven *overlapped*, and Brahms used to come to our house? We're Austrians. Viennese. Doctors come from all over the world to study here. Philosophers. Architects. A city of art lovers and intellectuals like no other.

LUDWIG   Yes, and don't forget the cafés, the cakes . . .

HERMANN   The seat of six hundred years of accumulating Poles, Czechs, Magyars, Romanians, Ruthenians, Italians, Croats, Slovaks and God knows what else, from the Swiss frontier to the Russian Empire, parliaments and parties in I don't know how many languages, stitched together by the same black-and-yellow livery of post boxes from Salzburg to Czernowicz and fealty to the

Emperor-King Franz Josef, who emancipated his Jews in time for us to grow up with the same rights as everyone else. Obviously prejudice doesn't disappear overnight. The civil service, the army, the university . . .

LUDWIG   No. That must be why the police stand around watching Jewish students get thrown down the university ramp, before arresting them for causing a disturbance . . .

HERMANN   Yes, that is why! But fifty years ago you couldn't get a foot in. You couldn't travel without a permit, or get a bed for the night in village or town except in the Jewish quarter . . . and of course you couldn't up-sticks to come and work in Vienna; but if you lived in Vienna you lived in Leopoldstadt, you wore a yellow patch, and stepped off the pavement to make way for an Austrian. By all that's holy, it happened in one lifetime. My grandfather wore a caftan, my father went to the opera in a top hat, and I have the singers to dinner—actors, writers, musicians. We buy the books, we look at the paintings, we go to the theatre, the restaurant, we employ music teachers for our children. A new writer, if he's a great poet like Hofmannsthal, walks among us like a demi-god. We literally worship culture. When we make money, that's what the money is for, to put us at the beating heart of Viennese culture. This is the Promised Land, and not because it's some place on a map where my ancestors came from. We're Austrians now. Austrians of Jewish descent! We're only one in ten but without us Austria would be the Patagonia of banking, science, the law, the arts, literature, journalism . . . The *Neue Freie Presse*, owned, edited and written by Jews, declined to notice its own literary editor's book—which you can have back now; thanks—because Herzl is a man with a beehive in his bonnet, a fantasy of the Jews of Europe and America uprooting themselves for a utopia among goatherds, which wouldn't even have a common language!

LUDWIG   Not Hebrew?

HERMANN Hebrew? You couldn't even buy a tram ticket in Hebrew!

LUDWIG Trams . . . that's a good idea.

HERMANN In fact, it's not a *Jewish* home for the Jews that Theodor Herzl has in mind, it's a liberal state where Jews can play cricket and tennis.

LUDWIG Really? Cricket?

HERMANN But who would want to go and live there?

LUDWIG Not many of us who are part of Austrian bourgeois high society, I grant you.

HERMANN But everybody who wants to be, will be! We're the torchbearers of assimilation. Your boy will wear the shako and fur-trimmed cape of an officer in the Hussars. What's the matter with you that you can't see what's happening?

LUDWIG But it's you who's missed it, Hermann. The only welcome Theodor Herzl's little book received was in the anti-semitic press. A state for the Jews? Good idea! Get them out of here! The Jewish press was offended, naturally. Written by middle-class Jews in the culture capital of Europe. They have enough trouble without Zionism making a song and dance of being different when sameness is the goal. But when we took Nellie to show the family, everywhere we went I was asked about Herzl. His book was going around like an infection. These are people whose parents arrived with *their* parents running for their lives from the Cossacks, and mentally they're living with their bags packed. In Galicia the Jews are hated by the Poles, in Bohemia by the Germans, in Moravia by the Czechs. A Jew can be a great composer. He can be the toast of the town. But he can't not be a Jew. In the end, if it doesn't catch up on him, it will catch up on his children. Ordinary Jews understand this. The Empire is made up of so many peoples you couldn't remember them all, but you left out the Jews, the only people without a territory. So when someone comes along and says, 'We lost our territory but we can have it again, a country where we're not on sufferance, where we can be what we once were . . . Where we can be warriors . . . '

HERMANN   They can have a territory. That's what assimilation means.

LUDWIG   I have to admire your patience on behalf of ordinary Jews. Meanwhile, the Christian Social party has got in on the anti-semitic vote. Our popular mayor is the orator of anti-semitism. We grew up in a liberalising time under a Liberal government which sincerely believed it represented millions when hardly any of them had a vote. Parliament was a gentlemen's debating chamber. But politics is no longer a gentlemen's game, so to hell with it. We worship culture! But, Hermann, assimilation doesn't mean to stop being a Jew. Your incidental effect would be the end of Judaism. Assimilation means to carry on being a Jew without insult. Episcopalians are assimilated. Zoroastrians are assimilated. I could be a Druid for all my professors care. It's only the Jews! I'm an unbeliever. I don't observe Jewish customs except as a souvenir of family ties. But to a gentile I'm a Jew. There isn't a gentile anywhere who at one moment or another hasn't thought 'Jew!' You can be baptised, you can marry a Catholic—

Hermann reacts.

Oh!—I didn't mean that the way it sounded—I didn't mean *you*— of course! I mean, I did but—I'm sorry. On one whisky! I'd better have another.

Hermann pours him a whisky. A short silence.

Are you really a member of the Jockey Club?

HERMANN   Willi von Baer is putting me up.

LUDWIG   Ah. I see.

HERMANN   The first Christian of Jewish descent.

LUDWIG   Ah. Progress.

HERMANN So what is your point?

LUDWIG About what?

HERMANN About anything.

LUDWIG Oh. It's gone. What's yours?

HERMANN Mine? Mine is that the twentieth century is upon us, and centuries don't come round again like the seasons. We wept by the waters of Babylon, but that's gone, and everything after, expulsions, massacres, burnings, blood libels, gone like the Middle Ages—pogroms, ghettos, yellow patches . . . all rolled up and dumped like an old carpet, because Europe has gone past them. Prejudice dies harder, but has the mayor physically harmed a single Jew?

At some point, Emilia has woken, without its being apparent. So her voice surprises the men, and also attracts Wilma's notice.

EMILIA Hermann, my dove, my firstborn! The goyim should give their right eye for what you turned away!

HERMANN What's that, Mama?

EMILIA Family! Jew-hatred is about nothing but blood and kin. They used to hate us for killing Christ. Now they hate us for being Jews. God give my grandchildren the desert!

LUDWIG Well . . . !

He raises his glass.

To a homeland for the Jews. Happy Christmas.

SCENE TWO

Gretl is alone, at a small writing desk, reading a note which she has just opened. She still has her outdoor coat on. Hilde lets in Hanna, dressed for the street, unhappy.

GRETL I've only just come in and found your note. I'm so sorry you had to—

27

HANNA (*overlapping*) I'm sorry I—

GRETL No, no, you were quite right to come, I'm all yours. Sit down, Hanna. Would you like tea?

HANNA Nothing.

Gretl dismisses Hilde.

GRETL Thank you, Hilde. So, tell me. What is it?

Hanna remains standing, fidgety.

HANNA I thought everything was going to go on just the way things do—

GRETL Fritz?

HANNA (*impatiently*) Yes—yes, of course, Fritz! Gretl, he was so— He was in such good spirits at the tea party, so nice about my dress, my hat—he couldn't have been more—you know what I mean, don't you?

GRETL He was charming.

HANNA Yes, he was. And sincere. You thought so too. We had a jolly time, didn't we? I was sure there would be a letter next day. Flowers, even.

GRETL And . . . ?

HANNA Nothing! I haven't heard from him at all! What should I do?

GRETL Oh, Hanna, I'm sorry.

HANNA (*tearfully*) I wrote my thank you, and now it's been more than a week, and I'm going home on Sunday.

GRETL Men.

HANNA What I think is he didn't understand my true feelings— his manners are so beautiful and he was being so amusing—reading those scenes with us—he was so funny—it's his way, you see, with anybody at all. He didn't realise I love him. I might as well have turned up in a glass case. I've decided to write to him. I'm sure it's best to tell him everything, and I've brought it to show you.

She takes a sheaf of handwriting from her bag and gives it to Gretl.

GRETL Ah.

HANNA (*anxiously*) Do you think it's too long?

GRETL He doesn't deserve you.

HANNA Yes, it's too long.

She snatches the pages back.

I knew it was. Will you write it for me? Perhaps he's ill. He might have been in bed the whole time with a fever. If only I could find Theodor.

GRETL Who?

HANNA (*snaps*) Theodor! His friend Theodor! I've gone to the Imperial every day for coffee and sat there hoping Fritz or Theodor would come in . . .

GRETL Sit.

She vacates her place at the writing desk. She places a card, pen and ink. Hanna sits at the desk.

'Dear Fritz. I'm going home on Sunday, so I've been thinking about my nice times in Vienna, and none was more fun than tea with you, so this is just to say thanks again, and if the army ever sends you to Czernowicz I hope you'll look me up. Your friend, Hanna.'

Hanna has written nothing.

(*firmly*) 'Dear Fritz.'

HANNA Oh, Gretl. I wish I'd just turned up on my own and let him take off my hat, my coat, and anything else he wanted. Everything would have gone differently.

GRETL It would, but you'd be sending the same letter.

SCENE THREE

Fritz's flat.

  FRITZ *and Gretl, post-coital. Fritz is in his twenties. She is half naked, wearing his military jacket.*

FRITZ I've had a letter from your little Jewess.

GRETL I'm going to go to hell for this. Catholic hell.

FRITZ Do you want to know what it says?

GRETL 'Thank you, goodbye, look me up if you're in Czernowicz.'

FRITZ That's incredible!

GRETL You should see her, Fritz, before she leaves. Make love to her.

FRITZ Don't say things like that.

GRETL If I give you back to her perhaps it will make up for stealing you from her, and I won't go to hell.

FRITZ You don't believe in hell.

GRETL I do now, now that I'm a sinner. You're my first big sin. I'm not going to come here any more. At least I won't have to live in terror of being seen. I don't know what's happened to me.

FRITZ I know what's happened to me. You didn't steal me, I stole you.

GRETL Yes, you did. I gave you no reason to pursue me, no reason at all. I was irreproachable. You were unforgivable. If Hanna wasn't such an innocent she would have noticed.

FRITZ There was nothing to notice on my end. I was correct. You started getting undressed. Yes, you did. You took off one

30

of your gloves. I ignored it. I poured tea and our hands met on the teapot handle. You took a puff of my cigarette. I thought any moment you were going to sit on my lap. Some chaperone!

GRETL Excuse me!—Who got Hanna to play so he could ask the chaperone to dance?

FRITZ I was being in character. Who got us reading scenes from your improper book? Some aunt!

GRETL (*stung*) I'm not her aunt! She's my . . . my sister-in-law's sister-in-law. I think. She's Hermann's sister's husband's little sister. Aunt. Honestly. I'm too old for you, that's true. I belong with Hermann, and I love him. I'm going home to show him I love him.

She is getting dressed now.

FRITZ Don't get dressed. Show me first.

GRETL No. I'm serious. You're my last gentile.

FRITZ You love me, don't you, Gretl?

GRETL I'm mad about you, but love is something else. It's just as well anyway because my portrait is nearly done, so I won't be able to keep disappearing for an afternoon. We will see each other here and there, won't we? Dinner parties . . . salons . . .

FRITZ Dinner parties? Salons? We don't get invited by the same people. It's a case of my people and your husband's people, baptised or not.

GRETL Concerts, then. Theatre.

FRITZ Is that how you met Hermann?

GRETL No, a hunting party at Prince Rotenberg's.

FRITZ Really? Is Hermann that rich?

GRETL Get dressed, Fritz, so you can find a cab for me.

FRITZ If he weren't baptised he'd have to be a Rothschild to get invited.

GRETL Please . . .

FRITZ You can't leave yet, it won't be dark for another hour.

She sighs, undecided.

There's time to say goodbye.

Gretl pushes him away. She decides. She starts tearing her clothes off.

SCENE FOUR

Night. Hermann, in white tie and tails, sits alone. The lamps are mostly unlit but there is some light on Gustav Klimt's portrait of Gretl, which is on an easel. Hermann is staring at it. The painting is not one of the spectacular portraits of a few years hence. It is closer to his portrait of Serena Lederer (1899) or of Marie Henneberg (1901–2). Gretl is wearing the green shawl.
  Ernst comes in, in an overcoat and tieless, carrying his 'doctor's bag'.

ERNST Hermann . . . are you unwell?

HERMANN No. I'm sorry if my message caused you anxiety. What do you think? We haven't decided where to hang it. Gretl favours the cloakroom.

ERNST Well, it's . . . not bad. I'm sorry Gretl doesn't like it. Is she all right?

HERMANN Oh, yes. She had retired when I came in. I've been out to dinner, Willi von Baer's boys-only dinner to celebrate his birthday.

ERNST Where did you go?

HERMANN It was at home. The Baron and Baroness were in the country, conveniently. There were twenty of us. I didn't know everybody. I knew half of them perhaps. A lot to drink. Dinner, cards, billiards . . .

ERNST (*puzzled, cautious*) Oh yes?

HERMANN We played poker, I won a huge hand, and I won it with a bluff, which I then showed, to some applause . . .

ERNST (*interrupting*) Hermann.

HERMANN Yes? What?

ERNST It's three o'clock in the morning.

HERMANN I know. Well, my opponent took it badly. But the moment passed, so I thought, and Willi proposed an adjournment to a certain house in Kärtnerstrasse where, he assured us, the ladies are regularly inspected for a medical certificate. The proposal was received with acclamation. I pleaded an early start. My opponent at cards then made an extraordinarily coarse joke which I need not repeat to you. But I should give you some indication. It concerned the very personal inspection a gentleman was required to submit to, to establish his bona fides at the more discriminating of such houses.

ERNST A comedian.

HERMANN Willi, who is a decent chap, gave me a smile and a shrug but our friend plunged on. Between the untouchable daughters of good families, he said, and the sweet young things of the working classes who were very likely to give you a dose, it didn't leave a man much, even if one took the view, which he did, that a Jewess is not a Jew. Laughter and cheers. No, he said, the best bets were the wives of the bourgeoisie, pretty young women who'd fulfilled their purpose by having a child or two and were now bored with nothing to do except take tea with each other— but best of all, he said, were the wives of rich Jews, factory owners and suchlike, because in Fritz's opinion—his name was Fritz, a lieutenant in the Dragoons—in Fritz's opinion, these wives were voracious for sex with a gentile, for anatomical reasons. I felt sorry for Willi presiding over such a gaffe. I was even sorry for Fritz, as though I'd watched helplessly a skier ski into a crevasse. I thought I'd better pull him out. 'My dear fellow,' I said, 'we haven't been properly introduced, it's Willi's fault.' 'Oh,' he said, 'I know who you are.' Dead silence. More fool me, eh?

ERNST What did you do?

HERMANN Obviously, I said, 'In that case, you will be hearing from me,' and I left.

ERNST Hearing from you? Oh no. Absolutely not. Because this idiot felt like insulting you over losing at cards?

HERMANN It was my wife he was insulting.

ERNST He doesn't even know your wife. It was you, and you should have socked him and have done with it.

HERMANN You don't understand anything. In matters of honour, we don't *hit* each other.

ERNST What 'we'?

HERMANN Don't be obtuse . . .

ERNST You're not 'we'.

HERMANN I'm not a gentleman?

ERNST Is this Fritz a gentleman?

HERMANN Of course. An officer and a gentleman. Character doesn't come into it. If I don't go through with this comedy I'll be a social pariah among my . . . my circle, friendships I value. I don't want to discuss it any more. I want this over with. Ernst, I have the honour to ask you . . .

ERNST (*panicked*) Why me?

HERMANN Because you're a doctor. These affairs might require a doctor. Who else could I ask? I want you to go and find the house in Kärtnerstrasse—

ERNST How on earth do I—?

HERMANN Ask a policeman. Willi's party will be there till morning. Request an interview with Baer. Present my compliments and ask Willi if he would do me the honour firstly of demanding an apology from his guest, failing which, secondly, to make the arrangements for a shooting match at first light with rules to be agreed on both sides.

ERNST No. Are you insane? How would I face Gretl?

HERMANN I must say I expected you to have a little more faith in me. I'm a very good shot.

ERNST Then you'd be charged with murder, and by the way I thought you were a Catholic—

HERMANN A Catholic, an Austrian citizen, a patriot, a philanthropist, a patron of the arts, a man of good standing in society and the companion of aristocracy. My great-grandfather was a pedlar of cloth. His son had a tailor's shop in Leopoldstadt. My father imported the first steam-driven loom from America. They strove to lift me high. Absurd as it is, I would be repudiating them if I flinched now.

ERNST Hermann, no offence, but don't you think you repudiated them by being baptised?

HERMANN No. They were Jews, they knew a bargain when they saw it.

Pause.

Do you mind if I take that back?

ERNST I would.

Hermann sighs, gestures helplessly.

HERMANN I can tell you the moment I decided not to be a Jew. My Grandpa Ignatz—Mother's father—told me when I was nine or ten how he once tossed a coin into the hat of a man playing a fiddle

35

on a street corner. The man stopped playing and said, 'Where's your manners, Jew?', and snatched Grandpa's cap off his head and threw it into the road. 'What did you do?' I said. 'Why, I picked up my cap,' Grandpa said. He had a good laugh about it. His hero was Bismarck. If he had been able to choose his life, he said, he would have been a Prussian aristocrat.

He pauses.

If this ends badly . . . I've written a note for Gretl. Otherwise, there is no need for her to know anything. I ask that of you.

He makes his last appeal.

Ernst . . . we're both Christians.

Ernst's answer, after a pause, is to pick up his bag and let himself out. Hermann stays still.

SCENE FIVE

Dawn.

Fritz's apartment. Fritz, holding a drink, is wearing his officer's dress uniform. Hermann has just entered.

FRITZ That was a damn good evening Willi laid on. (*Pause.*) I presume I may ask to what I owe the pleasure?

HERMANN It doesn't suit me for my wife to be made the object of scurrilous insinuations in the company of my friends. I will be satisfied if you admit the fault and apologise to me in writing, to include our understanding that I may show your letter to our host, and to anyone who was present, should I so choose.

FRITZ I don't recall saying anything that concerned you or your wife, Merz, and nothing that I need to apologise for.

HERMANN Then I take it that you mean to settle this business on the field of honour.

FRITZ (*amused*)   The field of honour! What romance have you been reading?

HERMANN   By God, I won't stand for this. Are you putting yourself at my disposal? One ball at twenty paces. A second ball at fifteen paces. I would consider myself satisfied.

FRITZ   I'm afraid I can't oblige you.

HERMANN   What do you mean?

FRITZ   I can't fight a duel with you. In my regiment an officer is not permitted to fight a Jew.

HERMANN   I'm a Christian.

FRITZ   This is painful for me.

HERMANN   I'm a Christian, damn you!

FRITZ   Let me put it this way. In my regiment, an officer is not permitted to fight someone whose mother was a Jew.

HERMANN   And damn your regiment!

Fritz throws his drink into Hermann's face.

FRITZ   Let's have no more of that. I ask you not to refer to my regiment.

Fritz takes a black walking stick with an ivory handle from an umbrella-stand.
Hermann stares in disbelief and makes a gesture as to defend himself.

A relic from my student days, if you're looking for a body to make remarks about . . . The sceptre of membership in the German-Austrian students' association. We had a manifesto, which declared, I'm afraid, that since a Jew is devoid of honour from the day of his birth, it is impossible to insult a Jew. A Jew cannot therefore demand satisfaction for any suffered insult. That's the gist of it. The swagger of braggarts, not to my taste, but there it is. You see what we're up against. I can't fight you, twice over!

Hermann is utterly at a loss.

HERMANN Then, how do you propose—? How am I to—(*A spurt of anger.*) Do I have to thrash you?

FRITZ Don't take everything so hard.

Fritz puts the stick back. He looks at Hermann amiably.

Do you know, Merz, you're the kind of Jew I like. Our mayor Handsome Karl says, 'I decide who's a Jew.' Good, don't you think? But I'm not the mayor.

Pause. Hermann has gone into himself. Fritz sighs.

I'll tell you what. I'll write you a letter as we're mutual friends with Willi, something to the effect that if I fell short of good manners as his guest, I regret it, and if anyone—no, if *you* were offended by my behaviour, I would hope never to repeat it in your presence. How does that sound?

Fritz settles himself where he might write. He gets busy. Hermann needs to sit down. He sits down.

Where do you know Willi from anyway?

HERMANN What?

FRITZ How do you know Willi?

HERMANN The races.

FRITZ Ah. The races. The Baron has a racing stable. Well, you'd know that, of course.

He is ready to write. He thinks for a moment, then starts to write.

Do you have horses?

Hermann's had the stuffing knocked out of him. He answers mechanically.

HERMANN No. I'm thinking of going in with Willi as an owner.

FRITZ   Ah.

Fritz has a doubt.

I thought the Jockey Club . . . oh, I see. Your money in his colours.

Hermann feels his dignity demands a defiant answer.

HERMANN   Willi is putting me up for the Jockey Club.

Fritz stops writing and turns to Hermann.

FRITZ (*amused*)   Don't be absurd. Did he tell you that? They'd chuck him out if he tried!

Fritz goes back to his letter. Hermann sits still. Fritz writes dashingly. Hermann notices a small book on the table next to him. He picks it up, surprised. He opens it, more surprised.

HERMANN   How do you know my brother-in-law?

FRITZ   Your brother-in-law? Who's that?

HERMANN   Doctor Ludwig Jakobovicz, of the University, the mathematics faculty. You have his copy of Schnitzler's new play, privately printed and inscribed to Dr Ludwig Jakobovicz.

Fritz stops writing and turns to Hermann again.

FRITZ (*pause*)   Ah. I know Hanna Jakobovicz, of course. I asked her to dance . . . somewhere. Miss Jakobovicz and your wife came to tea one day.

HERMANN   My wife?

FRITZ   Yes. Miss Jakobovicz brought your wife to tea.

HERMANN   My wife came here?

FRITZ   Didn't she mention it?

Fritz turns back to his letter.

Mrs Merz brought Schnitzler's play. It was fun. We read a couple of scenes. Miss Jakobovicz and I, then Mrs Merz and I, then I and Miss Jakobovicz, then I and . . .

Hermann sits still, thinking it through. Fritz signs his letter with a flourish.

There we are!

Hermann stands up.

Would you like to take the book? I ought to have—

HERMANN   No.

FRITZ   I should have returned it long ago.

HERMANN   I'll leave that to you.

FRITZ   Well, I could have it sent round, of course. I will not have the pleasure of seeing Mrs Merz, as far as I know.

He holds out the letter.

Would you like to read the letter?

HERMANN   No. It's not the letter I asked for, and in any case I don't want it now.

He gathers himself to leave. He hesitates.

I found it offensive that to insult me you should insult a woman you didn't know, whom you knew nothing about, who only existed for you as an abstraction. But I see that it was Gretl you betrayed with your filthy mouth. God forgive me that I should dine with men like you and think myself raised up in the world!

He is leaving, but hesitates again.

I don't want my wife to know I've been here.

FRITZ   She's your wife—up to you. You're a lucky dog, Merz.

Hermann leaves.

Emilia's voice speaking the Kiddush in Hebrew carries the transition into the next scene.

SCENE SIX

Seder.

At second glance—not at first—we note that Gretl's portrait is now hung on the wall.

The family are 'impossibly' crowded around the Merz table, all the more crowded because at the head of the table is a special chair with arms, stuffed with cushions. This is Emilia's place. She is flanked by Jacob and Pauli. Sally and Rosa are seated among Eva, Wilma, Hanna, Ludwig and Ernst—and Gretl and Hermann.

Jacob, Ludwig and Ernst wear yarmulkes. Hermann wears his everyday hat. Pauli wears an operetta officer's shako. Eva holds baby Nellie.

Hermann, Gretl and Ernst are 'guests'. Gretl is full of party spirit; the children likewise but also awed by the occasion.

The atmosphere of the meal is serious but celebratory. The Seder table is sparkling with candlelight on glassware and the best china and silver. The Seder Plate with its arrangement of symbolic foods is on the table with the plate of matzo breads and a bowl of salt water. Each person has a plate and a glass.

The Seder marks the beginning of the Jewish holiday of Passover. It is a reminder and a retelling of the story of the Jews' flight from slavery in Egypt, as told in the Book of Exodus. The Seder begins with a blessing (the Kiddush), spoken in this case by Emilia, and the first cup (glass) of wine. The blessing, spoken in Hebrew, becomes audible in the transition into Scene Six. When the scene is in place, the Kiddush continues seamlessly in English.

EMILIA (*concluding*) . . . Thou also separateth thy people Israel, and didst sanctify them with thy holiness. Blessed art thou, O Eternal, who maketh a distinction between holy and not holy. Blessed art

41

thou, O Lord, our God! King of the Universe who hath preserved us alive, sustained us, and brought us to enjoy this season.

> *Rosa has left her place to stand by Emilia with a small towel.*
> *Emilia 'washes' her hands in a special bowl of water and dries them, Rosa, proud and relieved, skips back to her place at table.*
> *During this, the first wine is drunk or sipped.*

For the benefit of the Papists, we now drink the first cup of wine.

ERNST   Good news!

WILMA   Ernst is Protestant, Emilia.

ROSA   It's just like apple juice!

SALLY   It *is* apple juice, fool!

ROSA   Fool yourself!

GRETL   Mine has turned into wine, it's a miracle! (*Faux pas.*) Oops!

EMILIA   You are all welcome, including Hermann and Gretl.

HERMANN (*drily*)   Thank you, Mama.

> *By now Emilia has taken the sprig of parsley from the Seder Plate and dipped it in salt water. Everyone gets a bit of the parsley.*
> *Meanwhile, Wilma and Ludwig share a moment. Wilma has a tear to wipe away. Ludwig presses her hand in sympathy.*

LUDWIG   I know, I know.

WILMA   Her big heart just gave out.

LUDWIG   Yes. Yes. (*Correcting with tact.*) Her kidneys.

WILMA   And Poppa's all alone.

LUDWIG   Half the village invited him to Seder.

WILMA   He's alone!

LUDWIG   Oh. Alone. Yes, well . . .

WILMA Not for long, though, if that hussy Malka Mabovich has anything to do with it.

HERMANN (*to Jacob*) Do you know what this is?

JACOB No.

HERMANN It's the bitter herb to remind the Jewish people of bitter days in the land of the Pharaoh.

EMILIA Blessed art thou, O Lord, our God! King of the Universe! Creator of the fruit of the earth.

ROSA I don't like it.

SALLY You're not supposed to!

ROSA I know!

PAULI Can I break the matzo now, Grandma Emilia?

EMILIA Pass it over, darling.

The plate of three layers of matzo bread is passed along.

LUDWIG (*formally*) This is the bread of affliction which our forefathers ate in and out of Egypt. This year we sit at the table half glad and half sad, here far away from our own land, but next year we hope to celebrate Seder in the land of Israel.

HANNA This year we are still as unhappy as slaves but next year we pray to be free and happy.

PAULI Can I now?

Given the nod by Emilia, Pauli breaks the middle layer of bread.

EMILIA The larger half of the broken matzo, called the afikomen, is customarily hidden away from the Seder table by one of the family. In this family the afikomen is hidden by the youngest child present. Step forward, Miss Rosa Kloster.*

---

* Dramatic license: normally, the afikomen is hidden by an adult for the children to seek. But it is not unknown—as here—for a family to customize their Seder.

GRETL Bad luck, Sally.

SALLY (*bravely*) She's younger by this much.

She indicates an inch between her finger and thumb.

Next year *I'm* going to be younger.

Meanwhile, Rosa has taken possession of the afikomen. We don't see where she hides it.

EMILIA Now, the second glass of wine.

ERNST Cheers!

Wilma rolls her eyes at that.

WILMA At least I didn't marry an Egyptian.

Rosa returns, gleeful.

ROSA I've hidden it!

PAULI Shhh!

EMILIA (*pointedly*) Now, which of you children has a question to ask?

HANNA This must be a new record for the Seder.

GRETL (*to Jacob*) Go on, darling, ask Grandma anything you like.

WILMA It's a Seder, Gretl, not 'ask me another'.

Pauli has had his hand up, terribly eager.

EMILIA Yes, Pauli?

PAULI (*formally*) Why is this night different from all other nights? Why on this night do we not eat bread as normally but only matzo? On all other nights we may eat all kinds of vegetables but on this night only bitter herbs . . .

The Seder continues but is progressively overtaken by the sounds of heavy artillery, machine guns and a military band playing the 'Radetzky March'.

. . . On other nights we do not dip in salt water but on this night . . .

The sound effects an ellipse in the ceremony.

EMILIA   There was a time when we were slaves of Pharaoh in Egypt but God brought us forth from there with his mighty hand . . . How terrible is the thought that our children and our children's children might still have been slaves to a Pharaoh in Egypt. Let us not say, then, 'We know the story well.' It is still our duty to retell the story of how we were brought out of Egypt . . .

Hermann has stood up and put his hat on his chair. In his own world now he cries out.

HERMANN   Gretl . . . oh, Gretl.

Gretl comes gaily to him. They dance together to the 'Radetzky March'.

Fade to black.

SCENE SEVEN

1924.

The Merz flat is not significantly altered in appearance. Gretl's portrait is in place. There is a gramophone with a horn, playing the Charleston.

Hanna's daughter Hermine (Mina), twenty-two, is dancing energetically, enjoying herself. She is, in a word, a flapper. Hanna, aged forty-three, is worrying over a music score. While Hermine dances, Poldi, now in her sixties, is unloading a tray on to the large table: two bottles of wine, a dozen glasses, and a selection of finger food. She then leaves with the empty tray.

In dumbshow, their words lost under the music, Sally, holding her infant baby, and her husband Zac, holding the baby's bottle, are in the middle of an argument, which continues as they leave.

Jacob, thirty-two, has come out of the war minus one eye and with one useless arm. He is reading a newspaper on a stick. He is disheveled, wearing his pyjama jacket instead of a shirt.

Nellie, twenty-five, is using scissors to cut and rip an Austrian Republic flag, removing the white middle panel of the red-white-red.

Two men are playing chess, just to pass the time. AARON Rosenbaum, a working-class intellectual, is Nellie's husband, a year or two older than her. KURT Zenner, in his forties, a respectably dressed philosopher, is the husband of Hanna and the father of Hermine.

KURT Hanna, my love, you don't have to stay.

HANNA But I'm the baby's auntie.

HERMINE Mum, we'll explain.

Encouraged by Hermine, Hanna gathers her things and discreetly departs.

Poldi enters with the empty tray, which she starts to load with everything on the table.

When the record finishes, Hermine collapses into a chair.

HERMINE I want to go to America.

POLDI First, *old* Mrs Merz wants the drinks and food served around her bed; next, *young* Mrs Merz wants the drinks and food in here; next, guess what, and I'm going back and forth like the Pressburg tram.

Somebody's been at the snacks.

NELLIE It's Jacob. I told him not to.

JACOB So I stole a knish.

Poldi exits with the loaded tray.

Now it becomes possible to hear raised voices and a crying infant from the further reaches of the flat.

Hermine gets up to go to the gramophone.

JACOB No, thank you.

Hermine compliantly turns the machine off.
Poldi returns with the loaded tray.

POLDI Guess what.

Poldi starts unloading the tray.

NELLIE What's happening in there, Poldi?

POLDI Miss Sally is having second thoughts—Mrs Fischbein, I mean.

HERMINE She already had second thoughts.

POLDI Now she's having them again.

HERMINE So are we on or off with the circumcision?

POLDI I think it's on again, I mean off. Your Aunt Eva says since Grandma Emilia invited everyone to have the *bris* here, and laid on the food and drink, it would be ungrateful of Sally not to go through with it.

JACOB (*scornfully*) Grandma Emilia invited everyone because she can't get out of bed and didn't want to be left out.

Rosa, thirty-one, a smart New Yorker, enters, making a beeline for her handbag.

ROSA I need a cigarette. Sally wants Dad to send out for gas so the baby won't feel anything. I think I talked her out of cancelling—we're *Jews*, for heaven's sake!—but she's still in two minds. She says how would Zac Fischbein like to be circumcised without anaesthetic. Zac says he liked it fine. He says he wouldn't have married her if he'd known there'd be an argument about it, and Mum says she wouldn't have married Dad if *she'd* known, and Dad says he isn't arguing and they should toss a coin. The Fischbeins are keeping shtum.

47

Rosa has taken a cigarette from a smart cigarette case in her bag, and she lights it.

JACOB   What's my mother saying, Rosa?

ROSA   Gretl says you'd forgotten all about your circumcision the next day.

JACOB   No, I think that was my baptism.

Rosa opens one of the bottles and pours herself a drink, ignoring Poldi's disapproval.

POLDI   The sooner the *mohel* gets here the sooner they'll all get over themselves and have done with it and enjoy.
No more tasting please, Mr Jacob. I waited in line for them and it's little enough to go round.

JACOB   They won't start till we're all here, anyway.

Gretl enters busily. She has aged well.

GRETL   Jacob! Why aren't you dressed?

JACOB   I am dressed, mummy.

GRETL   You're half-dressed—and where is your father? The *bris* is at four o'clock and the *mohel* will be here at any minute. (*to Poldi*) Poldi, those snacks are to stay in here.

She looks around in exasperation and hurries out again. Poldi leaves with the empty tray.

JACOB   Did you bring your dad, Nellie?

NELLIE   No. He might come on from . . . the doctor's . . .

AARON   Is Ludwig all right, Nellie?

NELLIE (*tersely*)   Yes, yes. He's not ill!

Jacob unkindly twigs.

JACOB Oh, Dr Freud, you mean. The most famous doctor in the world and they still haven't made him a full professor! Is that because his patients aren't ill?

NELLIE (*to Kurt*) Where's Aunt Hanna?

JACOB I'm talking to myself. Like Uncle Ludwig.

KURT She has a piano lesson.

HERMINE (*impatiently*) Oh, Daddy! (*Announces.*) Mum has a practice session for a recital at the Salzburg Festival!

NELLIE Oh . . . ! But that's wonderful, Kurt!

KURT To be strictly accurate, she's accompanying for a lieder recital, but it's a step into the limelight for her.

AARON (*mainly to Kurt*) The Salzburg Festival? The Republic nobody wanted trying to raise the corpse of Catholic Hapsburg Austria. Decorations will be worn. She'll be the only Jew in the house.

KURT You're talking nonsense. Salzburg is full of Jews during the festival, only they call themselves Social Democrats. But Hanna is married to a known Marxist, so she doesn't want to draw attention . . .

JACOB That's why she doesn't call herself Hanna Zenner.

KURT Exactly so. What's wrong with that?

JACOB I didn't say there was anything wrong with it. Handsome Karl is in his grave but the Christian Social Party lives on, a coalition of anti-Semites, with a Catholic priest as Chancellor, and every one a music lover!

ROSA You mean you're a Communist, Kurt?

KURT Only if we agree that the Bolsheviks are not.

ROSA It's all anyone talks about in the Village.

KURT   That's rather surprising.

HERMINE   She means Greenwich Village.

KURT   Ah . . . well, of course. In *my* village, I was the only Marxist.

HERMINE   Until Mum, but only till she bagged him. Is that how Nellie bagged you, Aaron?

NELLIE   Ha. He carried my books for a year, didn't you, my love?

AARON   I did, I fell in love with a bourgeois.

ZAC Fischbein, the distraught father of the baby, puts his head into the room.

ZAC   Did she come in here?

HERMINE   Who?

ZAC   Sally! She's disappeared. Did she go *out*? Oh, God! She took the baby!

Zac goes out.

ROSA   Oh, great. Zac!

Rosa follows Zac.

NELLIE (*to Aaron*)   Look outside.

KURT   I'll come with you.

Kurt follows Aaron out.

NELLIE   Or upstairs! Go and see, Jacob!

JACOB   Me?

He picks up his newspaper.

HERMINE   So it's off again.

But the baby is heard crying in the middle of a hubbub.

On again!

Rosa returns.

ROSA   Hiding in Poldi's room.

She refills her glass.

Anybody want one?

JACOB   Why not?

HERMINE   Why not?

NELLIE   No, thanks. We're not supposed to . . .

Rosa pours.
 Nellie separates the second red panel from the red-white-red.
 Jacob puts his paper aside.

JACOB   What are you doing, Nellie?

NELLIE   Making a red flag, what does it look like?

JACOB   It looks like you're making a *white* flag. Bespoke for the Austrian Republic. Except that we have no one else to surrender to. Except Germany, of course, but that's not going to happen. The French didn't fight the war so that Germany could end up bigger than before. What a triumph for the Peace Treaty, to re-draw the map of Europe so four million German-speaking Austrians wake up as Italians, Czechs, Poles, Yugoslavians . . . and here we are, leftover little Austria with the park benches chopped up for firewood, half starved and on its uppers because our coal is in Czechoslovakia and our wheat in Hungary. It was God's mercy on Franz Josef that he didn't live to see his Empire taken to pieces. Do you remember life in the old Empire, Mina, before the war?

HERMINE   We were rich, I remember that.

NELLIE   You're still rich compared to most people.

HERMINE   I'm not talking about most people. I'll know when I'm rich, thank you. I'm going to marry a banker.

ROSA   Watch out, I thought banks are collapsing all around.

HERMINE   Not those bankers, the other ones.

Nellie starts to sew the red panels together.

JACOB (*amused*)   Oh yes, the other ones. As perpetual outsiders, the Jews had no place at the table except to be the bank. If they'd had a country like most people, they would have developed a proper class structure. (*To Nellie.*) Given time, instead of having to join other people's revolutions you could rebel against your own ruling class. This could be a good time to start the whole thing off. Thanks to Russian pogroms and a Rothschild . . . I put that badly, but thanks to them anyway, the Jews have had a foothold in the Holy Land for a generation. Now with Palestine under a British mandate and Mr Balfour's promise of a homeland for the Jews . . . well, he didn't exactly promise, he said His Majesty's Government would look with favour upon, so long as the Palestinians—meaning the land without people for people without land—so long as the locals were all right with that—

ROSA   Jacob, stop it. By blood you're as Jewish as I am, so stop talking like an anti-Semite.

JACOB   Me?

ROSA   I know that noise. It followed me to America.

HERMINE   Will you take me back to America with you, Rosa?

ROSA   Yes, certainly, darling, if you have a degree in medicine and a job waiting, otherwise no.

JACOB   I'm a one-eyed cradle-Catholic of Jewish descent. That means I can offend anybody.

NELLIE What are your politics?

JACOB Those are my politics.

NELLIE Then you'll never love anybody.

JACOB I'm afraid not. Do you love the workers?

NELLIE Yes, I do. Do you think democracy in Austria stands a chance without them? There's no flag any more for the ground where we stood; liberal bourgeois Jews. It's the red flag or the standard of the old guard with fascism only a step away. Not even a step. Mussolini's frontier takes in what was Austrian territory only six years ago. Never trust a leader who likes dressing up. It means parliament is the next to go, and the Christian Socials like the cut of Mussolini's coat. There are more important things now than being a Jew.

JACOB The Jews will get blamed anyway—strikes, inflation, bank failures, Bolshevism, the black market, modern art. The Jews got blamed for everything before the war and when the war was lost they got blamed for that. War was going to make Jews Austrian once and for all, not just the assimilated, the baptised, the *mischlinge*, but even the refugees pouring in from Galicia and the Eastern Front. War fever made us all patriots. We offered up our lives to the Emperor. We didn't think he would take it literally, we meant just till Christmas when we'd won. But nobody was more pleased than Pauli when war was declared. Now a Jew would have a chance to rise in the regiment. So off he went in his shining white tunic with gold buttons and epaulettes and a plume in his shako, and his sash and tassels. What a target!

Nellie gasps, shocked.

HERMINE (*angrily*) Jacob!

Sally, Rosa's non-identical twin, carrying the crying baby, storms in, with Zac trying to calm her down.

SALLY I can't stand another minute of this. I'm all confused now. Zac hasn't set foot in a synagogue since his bar mitzvah, and suddenly he's quoting the Torah at me.

ZAC She's mad. We had a Jewish wedding!

Rosa comes to help.

ROSA Just hang on, Sally, the *mohel* will be here in a minute.

SALLY I don't *want* him here!

ROSA Let me take him, he's getting upset . . .

She takes charge of the baby, making soothing noises.

SALLY Mum never even sent us to Hebrew school, and now she says Nathan has to have his winkie snipped, poor little mite, so she can make her peace with Grannie Jakobovicz—who's dead!

Doorbell.

ROSA (*to Jacob*) If that's him, keep him in here.

SALLY I don't want to see him!

ZAC Of course you do . . .

ROSA Come along . . . It's all going to be all right . . .

Rosa, Sally and Zac leave with the baby, and Jacob leaves to answer the door. Nellie has taken no part in this, remaining within herself. Hermine is alert to her. She puts her arms round her . . .

HERMINE I'm sorry, darling, don't be upset by Jacob. He doesn't think.

Nellie nods, resisting her grief.

We'll always remember Pauli in his dress uniform, how happy he was, how happy we were being proud of him! I was in love with him from when I was little and he used to show us his toy soldiers lined up for battle, do you remember?

NELLIE (*trying to laugh it off*)   Of course I remember, you goose! He was the nicest big brother in the world.

The two young women take a moment of solace together.
Jacob, slightly ceremoniously, shows in Dr Floge.
Dr OTTO Floge is under forty, elegant, a bit of a surprise.

JACOB   I'm just going to put you in here, Doctor. We won't keep you long.

OTTO   Is your father home?

JACOB   Not quite yet, no. This is my cousin, Mrs Nellie Rosenbaum, and my cousin, Miss Hermine Zenner.

OTTO   Good afternoon.

NELLIE (*puzzled*)   Are you . . . ?

JACOB (*interrupting*)   Everybody's gathered in my grandmother's bedroom.

OTTO   Oh, yes? Why?

JACOB   She can't get up, you see . . . So you're a medical doctor, of course.

OTTO   Me? No. Law and economics.

JACOB   Really? So this is just a sideline for you . . . ?

OTTO   What is?

JACOB   The *bris*.

OTTO   What's that?

JACOB   The circumcision.
(*A seed of doubt.*) Are you Jewish?

OTTO   No.

Otto is unsettled. He tries to get things back on the rails.

I've brought some papers.

JACOB   There's *paperwork?*

NELLIE   For heaven's sake, Jacob. I'm so sorry, Doctor, it's a misunderstanding, my cousin Jacob is a numbskull.

JACOB   What?

NELLIE   We are expecting Uncle Hermann. Please sit down. Would you like a cigarette?

OTTO   Thank you, no, but if it's allowed to smoke I might have one of my cigars while I'm waiting.

He takes out a moderate cigar case.

(*To Jacob.*) By the way, we met once, before the war. Otto Floge.

JACOB   Sorry!

Sally enters with the baby.

SALLY   Right. It's on. Rosa talked me round.

JACOB   Really?

SALLY (*to Otto*)   This is my little Nathan. Thank you so much.

JACOB (*to Otto*)   Don't worry, I'll explain.
We're coming with you, Sally, to Grandma's room. Off we go, ladies.
(*To Otto.*) Have you got everything you need?

OTTO   Do you happen to have a cigar cutter?

SALLY   *What?*

OTTO (*unnerved by her*)   Well, don't worry, I can bite it off.

SALLY   Right, that's it! I'm taking the baby home.

NELLIE   Sally, wait!

Nellie gives chase.
The doorbell is heard again. Jacob leaves to answer the door.

HERMINE Ignore everything!

Jacob enters, followed by the Mohel, who carries his "doctor's bag."

JACOB This way, doctor

He checks himself.

You are a doctor of medicine, of course.

MOHEL Of course, what else?

Jacob leads him out.

HERMINE Are you in business with Uncle Hermann?

OTTO Not exactly. Just financial and legal affairs, very boring but all part of the bank's service.

HERMINE You're from the *bank*?

Otto has bitten his cigar. Hermine holds a match to it.

OTTO Thank you . . . Miss . . . ?

HERMINE Hermine. Families! I expect you've got a family yourself, so you understand.

OTTO Oh . . . yes.

HERMINE You have?

OTTO Oh—no, not really, just my parents.

HERMINE Dr . . .

OTTO Floge.

HERMINE Do you mind me asking which bank are you from?

OTTO Not at all. It's called Floge and Son.

HERMINE Would you like me to teach you to dance the Charleston?

OTTO Now?

Poldi enters with her empty tray.

POLDI   Guess what again.

She starts to load up the tray. Hermine helps, to speed her departure.

HERMINE   So Grandma Emilia had the last word . . .

POLDI   It was her dying wish, she said.

The front door is heard to slam.

At last.

Hermann comes in. Hermann is a well-preserved but now world-weary sixty-ish.

HERMANN   Otto! I'm so sorry.

OTTO   Don't concern yourself, I have been charmingly entertained by Miss Hermine.

Hermann intercepts Poldi on her way out with the loaded tray.

HERMANN   Oh, look at this, and no one has offered you a glass of something . . . !

He puts a snack into his mouth and picks up a bottle and two glasses. Poldi, affronted, leaves.

HERMINE   Have you forgotten the *bris* for Sally's baby? They're waiting for you in Grandma's room.

HERMANN   Please go and tell them to start without me.

Hermine gives a smile to Otto's bow, and leaves.

OTTO   My father sends his greetings. May I use the table for the papers?

Hermann busies himself with the bottle and glasses.
Otto moves Nellie's banner out of his way, bemused by it.

HERMANN   That must be Nellie's. My niece. She caught politics at the university, and now she goes on socialist picnics.

He hands Otto a glass and waves him to a chair.

Well, who would want to be a capitalist in Austria now? Revenue tax doubled. Income tax doubled. High tariffs and import restrictions all around us, new countries settling old scores with the Empire. Otto, Merz and Company has been through some times, believe me. We were making cloth from *nettles*! If you got caught in the rain in a Merz coat the coat got soggy and then fell apart. But we never stopped doing business, because we had the Empire to do business in. Fifty million people was a market. Six million people on the breadline is neither a market nor a tax base. We're living on the charity of the victors presented as loans we can't repay, and can't spend without the say-so of a League of Nations book-keeper sitting in Geneva. It's humiliating to be Austrian now.

(*entering*)

JACOB Poppa, the Jews are starting.

HERMANN Good.

(*Jacob nods and leaves.*)

The continuance of family custom is a respite. But it doesn't help Merz and Company, and I'll be damned if I'll be the Merz who failed to pass on a solvent business to his son. Did you meet Jacob?

OTTO He opened the door to me.

HERMANN The war soured him. It's a pity that girls are frightened off. He would have had a family, a son, one hoped, by now. I haven't said anything to him, by the way.

OTTO Is Jacob interested in the textile business?

HERMANN Not now, no. He's hollowed out. But give him time. I'm counting on having a good ten years to make myself emeritus.

OTTO But will he want to be you? I'm not being rude. It's a question.

HERMANN It's the family business. It's his turn.

Gretl enters at speed.

GRETL Hermann! What are you doing? You're missing it!

HERMANN So I'm missing it. Aren't you going to greet Otto?

OTTO Forgive me, Mrs Merz.

GRETL It's my first grandson's *bris milah*.

HERMANN What? He's not your grandson! He's Wilma's grandson. He's your . . . sister-in-law's sister-in-law's grandson.

GRETL (*to Otto*) He thinks I'm an idiot. It's my first *bris milah* for a grandson.

HERMANN (*to Otto*) There's a christening going on around my mother's bed.

GRETL A *christening*?

HERMANN Otto knows what I mean.

GRETL (*angrily*) Well, I do *not* know what you mean. (*To Otto.*) This is the baby's Covenant with God, and it's been going on with boy-babies ever since the first Covenant with Abraham, the first-ever Jew, only *he* was ninety-nine when God told him he had to circumcise his son and his servants, and that was when God promised Abraham and all his seed the land of Canaan everlastingly—Genesis, Chapter 17!

The baby, who had apparently fallen silent, now gives out a cry of surprise and pain.
Gretl also gives out a cry and dashes out of the room.

HERMANN She's discovered the Old Testament.

He contemplates Gretl's portrait for a long moment. Otto waits.
Ludwig enters in hat and overcoat, preoccupied, talking to himself, quite relaxed about it.

LUDWIG By Aristotle's law of the excluded middle, a statement is either true or its negation is true. Following Hilbert, we say, first, assume the Riemann hypothesis is false. If we can obtain a contradiction—

He notices Hermann.

Hermann!

He looks around.

Where is the *bris milah*? I was at the Doctor's.

HERMANN   Emilia's room. All well?

LUDWIG   *I'm* well. I'm not sure about the Doctor.

He leaves.

OTTO   Would you prefer to . . .

HERMANN   No, we're all right. The baby has to receive his Hebrew name, and there's a prayer and a blessing, and a celebration party. They'll be a while.

OTTO   I've prepared some projections for you to look at. The new Schilling will put a brake on inflation. If the Republic throws in its lot with an expanded Germany, the domestic market will expand with it, and the supply of raw materials—

HERMANN   What are you talking about? Union with Germany is forbidden by the Peace Treaty.

OTTO   The winners botched the peace, and they'll have to admit it. Besides, what can they do if the Republic votes for union? In the unofficial plebiscites in the Tyrol and Salzburg over 90 per cent voted to be German.

HERMANN   Alpine Austria! Backward-looking and hating everything modern, including Vienna.

OTTO (*lightly*)   Red Vienna is a provocation in a Catholic country. But today's modern is tomorrow's nostalgia. We missed Mahler when we heard Schoenberg, and we'd miss the Social Democrats if the Marxists took over.

HERMANN   My God, Otto, who might they be?

OTTO   Who might they not be? There are two ideas fighting for the soul of the working class: Marxism and nationalism. The class war turns people against each other, but nationalism binds them together. A quarter of a million Austrians voted for the German Nationals and gave us enough seats to make us the third party.

HERMANN (*surprised*)   You've joined the Greater German People's Party?

OTTO   A union of German speakers is the logical thing.

HERMANN   You'd give up Austria's independence just for logic?

OTTO   The Austrian and German peoples were betrayed in war, cheated by the peace, and beggared by reparation. We will restore our destiny together, as one nation, a Christian nation which leads the world in science and culture.

> *The faint sound of distant bombers begins to be heard.*
> *The baby has continued to cry. There is an outbreak of clapping, toasting, cheerfulness. Gretl enters, holding a glass of champagne.*

GRETL   The baby's name is Nathan! Nathan Shimon Ben Zacharia Fischbein! L'Chaim!

> *She leaves with the bottle.*
> *The bombers are getting louder, then very loud, flying over the city . . .*
> *Leaflets start falling from the sky. 'Gothic' print and swastika.*
> *A fourteen-year-old boy catches one of the leaflets. This is Nathan Fischbein. Sally is shouting to him.*

SALLY (*off*)   Nathan . . . ! Nathan! Get inside with you! Now!

> *The sound of bombers continues in blackout.*

November 1938.

The room is just different enough. The gramophone and Gretl's portrait have gone, along with some unspecified objects of value. The main difference, however, is in the implication of life without servants in an overcrowded space, cluttered with the personal belongings of travellers in transit—handbags, toys, shawls.

Once again, there are four young children.

BELLA and MIMI are the children of Sally and Zac. They are squeezed into an armchair, either side of Sally, while she reads to them from Grimm's tales. Zac is absent.

HEINI is the son of Hermine. He is the youngest and smallest. He is happily occupied plinking a toy piano on the floor. Hermine is sewing.

LEO, aged eight, is the son of Aaron and Nellie. Aaron has died. Leo is with Nathan and Ludwig, preparing to play cat's cradle.

Hanna is playing Hayden at the upright. Nellie is turning the pages of the old family photo album. EVA is presiding over a tea tray, and opening a box of patisserie biscuits.

A forty-ish Englishman in a well-worn suit, PERCY Chamberlain, has contributed the biscuits.

The flat is cold. Everyone is wearing extra clothes, shawls, etc.

Ludwig makes three double knots in a metre of string, spaced randomly, then ties the ends together to make a loop of the string for Leo to start off the cat's cradle.

Meanwhile:

SALLY (*reading*) 'The King chased the deer deep into the forest, and none of his huntsmen could keep up with him. Night was coming on when he stopped and looked around him, and he realised he was lost.'

NELLIE Who's this with you and Uncle Hermann, Mummy?

Eva examines the photo through her glasses.

EVA Annitchek . . . our nurse.
Look what Percy has brought us from Evian!

PERCY I'm afraid you would have preferred the loaf of white bread they stole from me at customs.

EVA Oh, don't! White bread!

NELLIE Thank you, Percy. Did you have a nice conference?

PERCY Splendid. The Royal Hotel at Evian-les-Bains is luxurious.* Lake Geneva was looking beautiful. Thirty-two countries attended. The immigration of Jews from Austria was the entire agenda, with hundreds of journalists taking notes. The only problem was, there was no story.

NELLIE Ah.

PERCY President Roosevelt's invitation to the countries taking part was at pains to make it understood that no country would be expected or asked to take in more Jews than was permitted under its existing legislation. So they weren't and they didn't.

NELLIE I could have told you that, Percy. Evian backwards spells naive.

PERCY Oh, I should have used that.

EVA So it was a failure!

PERCY Not at all, Mrs Jakobovicz. The conference met to do nothing and concluded that there was nothing to be done; so it was a success. The delegates explained that they were taking in as many Jews as the trade unions and the middle class would stand for. They didn't say stand for. And they didn't say Jews. Political refugees. But the British delegate said Jews. He said that according to some people the whole problem would be solved if only the gates of Palestine were thrown open, but the very idea was untenable, owing to the terms of the British mandate in Palestine, and prevailing conditions.

EVA I don't want to go to Palestine.

* A dramatic licence. The Evian Conference took place four months earlier, from 6 to 16 July.

NELLIE That's good, because the Arabs don't want you. The Arab revolt is the prevailing conditions.

PERCY Nellie knows. But you really have to go somewhere, you know, Nellie—

NELLIE In a minute, Percy . . .

She takes the box of biscuits and hands it around. Sally, Mimi and Bella each take one. Nellie humorously places a biscuit on Hanna's keyboard. Hanna snatches it off, while playing.

SALLY (*reading*) 'I have a daughter, said the Witch, who is as beautiful as any you will find. If you will make her your Queen, I will show you the way out of the forest.'

Meanwhile Leo has made the first cradle.

LUDWIG Stop there. We made three knots in the string. You see where they are?

It doesn't matter where the knots are.

Your turn, Nathan.

Nathan makes the next cradle.

Good. Stop again. Now where are they?

LEO There, there . . . and there.

LUDWIG Who'd have thought it? Your turn, Leo.
Good. Stop. Now look where the knots have gone.

During this, Nellie arrives with the biscuits, is greeted and thanked, and biscuit-munching finds its place, while Nellie takes her offering to Percy, who has found himself a chair.

PERCY (*privately*) Nellie, I can't stay long. I was at the British Consulate this morning—

Nellie is fond but helpless.

NELLIE   Oh, Percy . . .

PERCY   You really must, my darling.

NELLIE   I'll come back.

She returns to Eva to serve tea. Percy has brought a newspaper, the
Reichspost.

LUDWIG   Imagine the cat's cradle is in a glass box, and the string
is invisible except for the knots. Each knot has an address—so far
from *this* edge, so far from *this* edge, so far from *this* edge.

His finger moves along three edges of the imaginary box.

The knot is where the three lines meet: the three numbers, which
we call the co-ordinates, give you the address for each knot.

Ernst enters and takes a position.

ERNST   Behold!

*Ceremoniously, Ernst takes off his overcoat and jacket, and puts on the
overcoat.*
*They watch while Ernst proceeds to demonstrate how to fold a jacket,
beginning by turning the sleeves inside out. Nathan loses interest.*

NATHAN   Go on, Uncle Ludwig.

LUDWIG   If you didn't know it was cat's cradle, there seems to be
no rhyme or reason to the way the knots change their address. And
if I wrote down the addresses for you, how could you find the rule
that turns one set of three numbers into another set? You might as
well look for the rule that makes a fly go this way then that way.
But, as it happens, we do know, like God, that everything unfolded
from our game of cat's cradle. Each state came out of the previous
one. So there is order underneath. Mathematical order! But how
can we discover it?

NATHAN   The knots always stay the same distance from each
other, because we didn't cut the string. They're not allowed to
show up anywhere they like.

Ludwig points his finger at Nathan, almost like an accusation.

LUDWIG (*to Leo*) This is a mathematician.

NATHAN (*pleased*) Is that mathematics?

SALLY (*reading*) 'The King had already been married once, and by his first wife he had seven children, six boys and a girl . . . '

PERCY (*with his paper*) Sally's going to be out of a job, according to the *Reichspost*. From now on mixed race is going to count as Jewish . . . to be excluded from the professions, like Jews. No *mischlinge* in journalism, the creative arts, the performing arts, literature . . . Culture is *verboten*.

SALLY My sister's lawyer has written to the American Consulate. He says he's very hopeful for our visas if Zac says he's agricultural.

MIMI Go on, Mama.

Sally resumes reading.

PERCY In Berlin the Jews are still allowed to go to the cinema, the theatre, restaurants, cafés, to use the trams, the parks, to go shopping . . . As anti-Semites the Germans have some catching up to do on the Austrians.

Meanwhile, Ernst's jacket-folding is proceeding carefully, going back to the start when it goes wrong.
Hanna has been picking her way through the 'Gott Erhalte', the old Imperial anthem composed by Haydn and latterly appropriated for 'Deutschland, Deutschland über Alles'.

HANNA Oh damn them, damn them! They've stolen our old Imperial anthem for their bar-room singalong, and now all I can hear is 'Deutschland, Deutschland über Alles'!

EVA Well, don't play it.

HANNA Don't play Haydn?

Some kind of unseen frightening drama starts to become audible from elsewhere in the building. There are shouts, cries, bumps, crashes, breaking glass, boots on the stairs, two rapid pistol shots. Everything in the room freezes. Everybody is frightened.

Then Heini runs bawling for 'Grannie!' and sanctuary. Hanna scoops him up and puts him on her lap, quietening him against her breast.

Meanwhile, Nathan goes to listen at the door for a few moments, to the indistinct shouting from below.

The twins just wait, Bella sucking her thumb. Leo shuts his eyes.

The drama downstairs falls silent. Nathan leaves the room. Ernst resumes folding the jacket.

MIMI   Go on, Mama.

Sally resumes. In due course Heini returns to his toy piano.

SALLY (*reading*)   'She had learned witchcraft from her mother, and she turned the six boys into swans, which flew away over the forest.'

EVA   Couldn't you find a place for Sally in your office, Percy, a secretary or something?

PERCY   My office? The paper won't even pay for my charlady.

HERMINE   Ask Uncle Hermann. Jacob can find room in the factory office.

Hanna has resumed on the piano.

Nathan comes quietly back into the room. He is thoughtful beyond his years. He checks on Sally, touches her reassuringly as she reads. He reassures Leo similarly, and goes back to Ludwig.

Ludwig, Nathan and Leo resume, now with pencil and paper at the table. They remain absorbed.

Nellie delivers Percy's cup and is thanked.

PERCY   Please sit down, Nellie. Say you will.

Everybody is occupied now—Eva with the photos—and the piano creates a bubble for Nellie and Percy to talk together. Nellie takes his hand and sits down next to him.

NELLIE Oh my dear Percy. Thank you. But I'd be leaving Mummy and Papa as if I'd drawn the lucky lottery ticket.

PERCY No, they'll get visas as your dependants. You and Leo will be British, which means Ludwig and Eva—

NELLIE I know what you think it means, but they won't leave. And things will calm down. Maybe the schools will open again for the Jews—

PERCY No, things will get worse—

NELLIE How can it be worse? Yes, we could end up in the ghetto like a hundred years ago—

PERCY Much worse.

Nellie, irritated, responds strongly.

NELLIE Well, I've *had* worse. I've had the walls blown out by artillery when our own Austrian army fired on the workers' flats and killed Leo's father.

PERCY But this is worse.

Tactless. Nellie returns to her chair.
Ernst has made a perfect square out of his folded coat.

ERNST Look at that. That's how an Englishman's valet folds a jacket to pack it in his trunk.

PERCY Is it? That's news to me.

ERNST It's what they teach you at the school for butlers and valets just started up. There's a rumour that the British Consulate is going to let in Jews in domestic service, because of the army taking what there was.

PERCY But you're not a Jew.

ERNST If they're giving visas I'm prepared to consider it.

EVA I heard it was Nobel Prizewinners.

ERNST No, it's domestic servants and Sigmund Freud. Did you hear about that, Ludwig?

LUDWIG What?

ERNST Dr Freud has gone.

LUDWIG Who?

ERNST Dr Freud. Gone.

LUDWIG He's dead?

ERNST No. He and his family got exit permits to England. I saw one of his patients at the butler school, hysterical agoraphobia. We were laying a table together. Well, permit me to state that I thought Freud was on to something from the beginning. The evidence was there to see, in the work of writers and artists. Ludwig!—long shot now—do you remember Klimt's 'Philosophy' painting? You were dragged into a row when it was exhibited in Paris. *Le goût juif*, the French said.

LUDWIG I remember Paris very well. I danced with a girl who danced with Riemann.

EVA You danced with a girl whose mother danced with him.

ERNST Didn't come off, never mind. (*To Percy.*) Klimt did three paintings for the university ceiling: 'Philosophy', 'Medicine', and 'Jurisprudence'. Bad dreams in each case. Sex and death. Pudenda, skulls, a giant octopus, beautiful priestess girls, everything floating, swirling, entangled. Scandal! The mayor, *Schöne* Karl himself, wanted to know whether the Minister of Culture was supporting art which decent Austrians found nonsensical and offensive. *Le goût juif*, in other words. Freud stayed out of it. But, by God, it was all

70

there. A dream is the fulfilment in disguise of a suppressed wish. The rational is at the mercy of the irrational. Barbarism will not be eradicated by culture. The last time I saw Freud, the most profound man I know, I asked him, 'Yes, but *why the Jews?*' He said, 'I don't know, Ernst. I wasn't going to ask you, but—*why the Jews?*'

HERMINE   Aren't you going to divorce Wilma, Ernst?

ERNST   Divorce Wilma? What an idea!

HERMINE   Nobody would blame you. I don't blame Otto. It was me or the bank.

SALLY   Mina!

HERMINE   Just saying.

MIMI   What, Mama?

Sally returns to the children's book. Bella is sucking a thumb, a cherished rag in her fist.

SALLY   Are you going to let me wash that, Bella?

Bella shakes her head vigorously, sucking.

MIMI (*solemn*)   She won't. Go on, Mama.

SALLY (*reads*)   'Just as the sun was setting, she heard a rustling of wings, and saw six swans come flying through the window.'

PERCY   Where is this school for butlers?

ERNST   The Athena apartments, third floor.

NELLIE   Are you going to write it up?

PERCY   I might take a look on my way home.

ERNST   You'll find a lot of bankers and stockbrokers wearing aprons and learning how to balance trays of glasses.

PERCY   Well, you must tell Hermann. It's not going to get better. Tell Jacob. You have to go. All of you.

EVA Ludwig and I are too old for another upheaval. We're all living on top of each other since the Nazis Aryanised our building, but you don't understand, Percy, we're used to this.

PERCY What do you mean, used to it?

EVA When Grannie Emilia was little she walked from almost Kiev to Lvov after their village was burned down. It will pass, and something else will take its place.

Percy is speechless with exasperation.

LEO Am I a mathematician, Grandpa?

LUDWIG Can you add up all the numbers between one and . . . twenty in your head?

Leo applies himself to this.

ERNST Have you thought of Shanghai, Eva?

EVA Shanghai?

ERNST Yes. They say you don't need a visa or a work permit for Shanghai.

EVA Shanghai??

ERNST There's boats from Trieste. You can book a passage, and apply for a transit visa.

EVA *Shanghai*?! I don't even like the food.

ERNST Ah, well. It's what I'd do if Wilma could get about.

PERCY (*angry*) This is all topsy-turvy. There are thousands leaving every month. The Office of Jewish Emigration can't get rid of the Jews fast enough. If the Swiss opened their borders, Eichmann would run special trains for you.

EVA Yes, for people with Swiss bank accounts; they can leave as soon as they've coughed up. Or people with family abroad, or who work for foreign companies, they can all leave as soon as they've paid the escape tax and the levy on everything they own. If they can get a visa, yes, the Germans will let them leave after robbing them of everything they had. Not everyone is willing to play their game. By a miracle Hermann has kept the business going through war, revolution, inflation, and now *Anschluss*, and saved it for Jacob. Why give it all away now?

PERCY   The Nazis will take it sooner or later, and put an Aryan in to run the factories, but Jacob shouldn't wait for that.

EVA   Don't you be too sure. Gretl is pulling strings—she's known the Chancellor since he was a boy.

PERCY (*incredulously*)   Hitler?

EVA   No, the new man in the Ballhaus. Gretl knows his mother.

PERCY (*almost losing his temper*)   Bürckel isn't Chancellor, he's the Reichskommissar of a province of the Third Reich formerly known as Republic Austria!—and now that's gone after only twenty years. What were you doing until the day German bombers flew over like an overture to Hitler's triumphant entrance into Vienna?

Heini puts his hands over his ears and makes a loud droning bomber noise. Percy desists. Heini desists.

HERMINE   It's all right, Heini.

Heini 'plays' his piano.

NELLIE   Do you mean us Jews?

PERCY   No! You socialists and social democrats!—when the Christian Socials got rid of parliament and invented Austrian fascism! Well, it wasn't enough to keep Hitler out! (*More calmly.*) Forgive me. When the paper sent me here, the man from *The Times* said, 'Percy, let's go to Graz, there's an NSP march.' I said, 'I thought the Nazis were illegal here.' 'Oh, they are!' So we went to Graz and saw twenty thousand National Socialists with swastika buttons marching through Graz, watched by delirious crowds and a few policemen. I said, 'Douglas, what are the Austrians doing about this?' 'These *are* the Austrians,' he said.

HANNA (*stands up*) My husband is in Dachau. I don't know if he's alive. So, no, I do not forgive you.

Quietly enraged, Hanna makes for the door.

LEO Two hundred and ten!

HANNA Ludwig, would you please *shut up with the numbers*!

Hanna continues out. Ludwig gives his teacup to Leo.

LUDWIG The answer is correct, but sadly—

Hanna re-enters at speed and continues across the room collecting Heini on her way.

HANNA Trouble.

She deposits Heini on Hermine's lap and sits at the piano, turning to face the room. The trouble arrives: a CIVILIAN wearing a long belted coat, a soft hat, a swastika armband, and carrying a briefcase.
Ernst stays standing, nervous. Ludwig stands up, frightened. Percy remains sitting. Nellie moves nearer Leo and stands, frightened. Eva remains sitting. Sally remains sitting, squeezed between her two children.
The Civilian looks round and picks on Eva. He does not shout but speaks curtly and too loudly.

CIVILIAN Get up. You're not at home now.

Eva stands up. Hanna stands up. Sally extricates herself from the children and stands.
The children: Leo watches everything without reacting. Heini puts his hands over his eyes. Bella whimpers, sucking furiously. Mimi stares, bleakly hostile.
The Civilian opens his briefcase and takes out a sheaf of papers. He takes a pencil from his pocket. He has noticed Percy—that Percy doesn't fit—and has to decide what tone is required here.

(*To Percy.*) And who are you?

PERCY A friend of the family. (*Gets to his feet.*) Percy Chamberlain. *News Chronicle.*

CIVILIAN English?

PERCY Yes.

Percy takes his passport from his pocket and offers it.

And you are?

CIVILIAN Watch your lip! Do you think I give a shit about English journalists? I can wipe my arse with your accreditation any time I like.

It terrifies everyone.

Stand still!

The Civilian checks the passport and the enclosed press pass, and returns it.

What are you up to in this nest of yids?

PERCY I'm having tea with my fiancée's family.

CIVILIAN Oh, your fiancée! Race defilement runs in the family. Where's Hermann Merz?

PERCY I don't know.

CIVILIAN (*to Nellie*) Where is he?

NELLIE He goes every day to St Joseph's Hospital to see his wife.

CIVILIAN (*caustically*) See her? Through the window?

NELLIE To ask after her.

CIVILIAN Elena Rosenbaum, widow. Widow of Social Revolutionary Aaron Rosenbaum. Fiancée?

Nellie hesitates, nods.
 Leo, still holding the cup, stands by.

And spawn, yes?

NELLIE   He's my son, Leopold.

The Civilian approaches Leo.

CIVILIAN   Leopold Rosenbaum.

Leo drops the cup, whcih shatters on the floor. The rhythm freezes. Leo awaits his fate.

Pick it up.

Leo jumps to it, collecting the broken pieces into his hands, and stands up. The Civilian turns aside and pokes his pencil at Ludwig.

CIVILIAN   Ludwig Jakobovicz?

LUDWIG   Professor Doktor Ludwig Jakobovicz.

The Civilian takes Ludwig's cap off and throws it down.

CIVILIAN   You address me as Herr Doktor.

Pokes his pencil at Ernst.

ERNST   Professor Doktor Ernst Kloster, Herr Doktor!

CIVILIAN   You're not a Jew. What are you hanging about for?

ERNST   I'm . . . family, Herr Doktor.

Next, Eva.

EVA (*shakily*)   Eva Jakobovicz, Herr Doktor. Hermann Merz is my brother.

CIVILIAN   A profiteer Jew making uniforms for soldiers to die in. Did you think you were Austrians, you old parasite bitch?

EVA   My son Pauli gave his life for Austria, and he was proud to do it. My wedding ring is iron since I gave my gold ring to the Emperor's war fund. Herr Doktor.

CIVILIAN   So one less Jew.

The Civilian points his pencil at Sally.

SALLY Estelle Fischbein, Herr Doktor.

CIVILIAN Is this your litter? Hello. Peekaboo. Hello, piglets.

He pokes his pencil into Bella's rag and pulls at it. Bella bawls. Sally gets among them, soothing them.
The Civilian turns his attention to Nathan.

NATHAN Nathan Fischbein, Herr Doktor.

CIVILIAN Zacharia is your father?

NATHAN Yes, Herr Doktor.

CIVILIAN You know where he is?

NATHAN He's at work, Herr Doktor.

CIVILIAN Correct. He's cleaning latrines at the barracks.

The Civilian pokes his pencil at Hermine.

HERMINE Hermine Floge, Herr Doktor. My son Heinrich.

Hanna is next.

CIVILIAN Hanna Zenner. I know you.

Hanna shakes her head.

Yes, I do. I know you by your concert name. You're Hanna Jakobovicz. Well, that's all over for you.

He looks around and sees that Hermann has come in.

HERMANN I am Hermann Merz.

CIVILIAN *(raising his voice)* *Umzugshauptmannsleiter* to you! Again.

HERMANN I am Hermann Merz, *Umzugshauptmannsleiter*.

CIVILIAN I was about to have you brought in.

The Civilian counts with his pencil.

Somebody is missing.

ERNST My wife is here but she's bedridden, Herr Doktor.

CIVILIAN Get her in.

ERNST She can't . . . she's—

CIVILIAN Get her.

SALLY She can't walk, Herr Doktor.

CIVILIAN In here.

Ernst goes out.

(*Impressed.*) Hanna Jakobovicz! Play us something while we're waiting.

Hanna starts playing something melancholic.

No, play '*An der schönen, blauen Donau*'.

Hanna plays 'The Blue Danube'. The Civilian hums along.
After some time, Ernst brings in Wilma in a wheelchair. Sally goes anxiously to her mother.

(*To Hanna.*) Did I tell you to stop?

Hanna resumes. Ernst wheels Wilma forward.

(*To Wilma.*) How are you feeling today, Mother?

ERNST She can't speak, Herr Doktor

CIVILIAN She can't *speak*?
Is that right, darling?

ERNST She can't hear, Herr Doktor

CIVILIAN Well, she can't do much!
So—pay attention!

He silences Hanna.

This apartment has been requisitioned by the Reich Housing and Relocation Office. You will each be allowed to remove personal

78

possessions in one suitcase, maximum weight thirty kilos, no item to have a value of more than fifteen Reichsmark. You will present yourselves outside the street door at tomorrow noon with your belongings. I am issuing you with transport dockets which you must show to the transport officer.

The Civilian brings the dockets out of the briefcase and goes along the line, handing them out, name by name.
He leaves Wilma out. Ernst, anxious, raises his hand.

(*To Ernst.*) Your wife needs to be in hospital.

ERNST   Yes, but . . .

CIVILIAN   I'll arrange an ambulance. Get her ready.

The Civilian has a docket just for the occasion. He scribbles on it and signs it.

You give this to the driver.

ERNST (*looking at the form*)   Steinhof is a mental hospital, Herr Doktor.

The Civilian turns to Hermann.

CIVILIAN   You can sit down.

He has a document for Hermann.

Read and sign.

Hermann takes out a spectacle case.

You don't need your glasses. Just sign it. You agree that the Merz Company, the mills, the factories, the entire business, owes its existence to your practice of fraud, tax evasion and theft, and you further agree that ownership is transferred to the state, without compensation.

Eva and Nellie in particular understand the tragedy of this.
Hermann takes out a fountain pen and signs.
The Civilian takes back his document and puts it in his briefcase. He also takes Hermann's pen.

He is ready to go, buckling the briefcase. Ernst steps forward.

ERNST   Herr Doktor, I must go with her! I understand her. No one else . . .

CIVILIAN (*shouts*)   Must? Must? There is no must any more!

The Civilian strides out.
    Leo gives a little cry. He is still holding the broken cup in his cupped hands, and he has hurt himself. He has been unconsciously gripping the broken cup. Now blood is dripping from his fingers. The cut is between his thumb and forefinger and it's not trivial.

NELLIE   He's cut his hand on the cup! Let me see, darling.

ERNST (*to Nathan*)   My bag.

Nathan hurries out. Leo sobs.
    Gretl now enters. She is wearing an old fur coat, cloche hat, and slippers. She uses a stick, an elegant cane. She is frail, with a tattered glamour.

HERMANN (*solicitously*)   What are you doing here, Gretl?

GRETL (*laughingly*)   I've got nothing on!

She shows Hermann inside her coat, discreetly.

The nuns wouldn't give me my clothes.

HERMANN   Well, don't worry. We can go back for them. But, my love, you must do what the doctor says.

Nathan hurries in with Ernst's doctor's bag. Everything is busy around Leo. Eva sacrifices her handkerchief for a swab. Ludwig collects the broken cup. The three children look on in awe. Ernst opens the bag, making light of the injury for Leo's sake.

ERNST   A couple of stitches, that's all!

Percy withdraws and starts making notes in a small notebook.
    Hermine breaks down. Hanna embraces her.

HERMINE   This is how they are with us. Daddy must be dead.

HANNA Come on, Mina, now, now . . .

Sally goes to Wilma and holds her hand.

GRETL What's happened?

HERMANN Listen, Gretl, put some clothes on and I'll take you
back to the hospital. Be good, now.

GRETL Where's Poldi?

HERMANN There's no Poldi any more, Poldi died.

GRETL Oh dear.

*Ernst has things to do. He lays out a couple of small bottles, cotton
swabs, needle, thread, a dressing. He sterilises the wound with iodine.
He threads the needle. The children draw closer, interested, and tell each
other: 'It was the cup, he's bleeding.'*

HANNA (*to Hermine*) We'd better get ready while we can still see
what we're doing. Come on, bring Heini.

GRETL I've got such a headache.

HERMANN What were you thinking of?

GRETL I wanted to find a synagogue.

HERMANN A synagogue? What for?

*Hermine takes Heini and goes out. Hanna pauses to offer sympathy to
Hermann.*

HANNA There was nothing you could have done, Hermann.

GRETL I've been thinking of having Hebrew lessons.

HANNA You might as well if you're staying. It's Hanna. How are
you, Gretl?

GRETL Hanna. Can you forgive me?

HANNA Forgive you? For what?

GRETL   No . . . it's gone.

Sally comes forward, frightened.

SALLY (*to Gretl*)   We're being thrown into the street. (*To Hermann.*) Where will we go?

HERMANN   Leopoldstadt.

Sally returns to gather up Mimi and Bella.
   Gretl looks to Hermann.

Sally.

GRETL   Oh, Sally.

HANNA   Why do you want to learn Hebrew?

GRETL   Why? What a question! (*To Hermann.*) Would you have married me if I was Jewish?

HERMANN   What is this nonsense? (*To Hanna.*) Ask Eva to come.

Hanna goes to comply. Ernst is ready to stitch.

ERNST   You'll hardly feel it, Leo.

First stitch. Leo yelps and cries. Nellie holds his other hand.

Good boy.

SALLY (*to Nathan*)   Come and help . . . you can have a suitcase, too.

MIMI   I didn't like that man.

NATHAN   Nor did I, but don't worry, Mimi, he isn't coming back.

Eva comes to Hermann and hugs him.

EVA   Oh, Hermann! I'm so sorry!

GRETL (*pleased*)   Eva!

EVA   Did they send you home, Gretl?

GRETL No, I escaped!

She shows Eva inside her coat.

HERMANN Put some clothes on her . . . and shoes.

Eva catches on.

EVA Come on, Gretl.

GRETL What happened to your Pauli?

EVA The war.

Eva takes Gretl out. Ludwig has taken charge of the broken cup.

LUDWIG (*to Hermann*) Thank you for having us. (*To Nathan.*) I can mend this. Have we got glue?

He follows Nathan and the children out.

SALLY We'll still be together, won't we, Uncle Hermann, until our visas come through?

HERMANN Maybe in one room.

Sally goes out.
    Ernst has been stitching, five stitches. Leo is crying.

ERNST All done! Good boy.

Ernst is still busy: antiseptic gauze, a bandage.

NELLIE Thank you, Uncle Ernst.

Percy pockets his notebook.

PERCY (*to Hermann*) Do you know about Ernst vom Rath?

HERMANN No, who's he?

PERCY A diplomat in the Reich Embassy in Paris. A Jew shot him this morning.

HERMANN (*after a beat*) Walpurgis night, then.

PERCY More than likely.

He goes to Nellie.

I'm going now. I have a confession, Nellie. We're getting married at the consulate tomorrow morning, eleven o'clock. Then we'll see.

NELLIE Yes.

PERCY You're a brave boy, Leo.

He shakes hands with Hermann.

Will you talk to Eva? Hitler wants a city without Jews, and one way or another he'll get it.

He leaves.
   Nellie comes to Hermann with Leo.

NELLIE I'm so sorry, Uncle Hermann.

Hermann kisses her.

HERMANN Look after Eva.

NELLIE She won't leave.

HERMANN We'll see, but Percy's right. You have to go while you can.

Nellie hugs him, and takes Leo out.
   Only Ernst, Wilma and Hermann are left now. Ernst finishes packing up his bag.

Ernst, will you see Gretl back into hospital? I'll come as far as the entrance.

ERNST (*nods*) Best place, at such times.

HERMANN She won't be coming out again. It's gone to her brain.

ERNST I'm sorry, Hermann. I'm sorry about everything, the family business . . .

HERMANN Between you and me, that was nonsense. The business isn't mine to sign away. It's Jacob's. I transferred everything to him in '36 when Austria and Germany signed the Friendship Treaty!

ERNST What difference does that make?

HERMANN It makes all the difference now because—it turns out—Jacob is a goy.

ERNST No, he isn't.

HERMANN Yes, he is. It turns out Gretl got pregnant by a goy and had Jacob.

ERNST My God. That must have come as a shock.

HERMANN Not really—it was my idea.

ERNST What was?

HERMANN That nine months before Jacob was born, Gretl had a fling with a Dragoon.

ERNST A military officer?

HERMANN Top drawer. Jacob's more Aryan than you are.

ERNST (*bewildered*) Wait. Does he exist, this Dragoon?

HERMANN Of course. He's written a letter, notarised. Jacob's Certificate of Reich Citizenship was Gretl's last bravo.

ERNST (*flounders*) You mean Gretl persuaded . . . found someone . . .

HERMANN Fritz was my idea, too.

Ernst thinks about this.

ERNST So he turned out a decent fellow.

HERMANN No, a real shit, I had to pay him a fortune. But my son will carry on the business.

ERNST Well!

He puts out his hand.

HERMANN You have to let Wilma go, Ernst.

After a hesitation, Ernst nods. Hermann now shakes Ernst's hand.
    Ernst goes to attend to Wilma.
    Heini comes in. He wants his piano.

Now let's see. Who are you?

HEINI Heini.

HERMANN You're my . . . sister's husband's sister's grandson, Heini.

He leaves.
    Ernst 'tidies up' Wilma. Heini ignores him. He starts to 'play' his piano.
    There is a distant shouting, then lorries approaching, full of shouting men, then, not far away, a shop window breaking, and more glass breaking as the shouting becomes clearer: 'Ju-da verr-rrecke!'—'Perish Judah'—as the lorries speed by, getting further away, glass breaking, and more glass breaking.
    Heini puts his hands over his ears.
    Ernst investigates his doctor's bag.
    He takes items out. He fills a syringe.
    He kisses Wilma on her forehead.
    Fade to black.

SCENE NINE

1955.
    Nathan is making a statement to an unseen committee. We see only Nathan. He is standing, wearing a rumpled suit.

NATHAN My name is Nathan Fischbein, of the University of Vienna mathematics faculty. I was born in 1924, the only son of Zacharia and Estelle, known as Sally. We lived on Schwarzenbergplatz, not far from the Merz apartment. Hermann Merz was my great-uncle by marriage, meaning that my grandmother's brother, Professor Doktor Ludwig Jakobovicz, was the husband of Hermann's sister Eva. I was often at the Merz apartment before the family was evicted on November 9, 1938, Kristallnacht, the 'night of broken glass'. I saw the portrait of Margarete Merz many times, hanging on the wall of the apartment. I called Mrs Merz Aunt Gretl. The first days of the *Anschluss* were indescribable. Mobs of—I would say—ordinary Viennese citizens forced their way into the homes of Jews and stole or smashed anything that caught their eye. I cannot say who took the painting. There were six or seven men who came in and took things, spitting at us and calling us filthy names. The Germans stopped this sort of thing happening after a week or two. It was too anarchic for them, they wanted to rob us in an organised way, they wanted first pick. I left Vienna with my parents and my sisters, Mimi and Bella, on one of the first transports to Theresienstadt in 1942; and the next year to Poland, directly to Auschwitz. My mother and my sisters were gassed immediately. My father died on the death march when the Nazis abandoned the camp with their prisoners, in January 1945, and—well, I don't want to get off the subject. I didn't see the 'Portrait of Margarete Merz' again until I saw it on public display at the Belvedere art gallery after the war. At the Belvedere the picture was called 'Woman with a Green Shawl', but there was no doubt it was the portrait of my Great-Aunt Gretl, who died from cancer in December of 1938.

Unsettlingly, Nathan starts to laugh but after a few moments it becomes clear that he is laughing in the Merz apartment, in the presence of Rosa and Leo.

'I don't want to get off the subject'!

The room is altered and unaltered. The Merz flat has been half stripped, and has been empty for years. Nathan and Rosa are just re-discovering it.

Smoking is allowed. Rosa has a box of patisserie from Demel and a Thermos flask with three cups in front of her. She is sitting where Grandma Merz was sitting in 1899, and where Eva was sitting in 1938. The first part of the scene incorporates the consumption of tea and cakes.

Rosa is sixty-two, and still a New Yorker, smartly turned out from hair to shoes, rings on her fingers.

Leo is a boyish twenty-four, a middle-class Englishman with a good haircut, comfortably dressed in jacket and flannels. His 'public school' accent is a little dated.

Nathan is thirty-one but seems older. He speaks English with a light accent.

Rosa and Leo wait for him to contain his laughter.

ROSA Well, you *were* getting off the subject. What's wrong with that?

NATHAN (*recovers*) You'd have to be there.

ROSA I *was* there.

NATHAN Not there. There.
(*To Leo.*) Can you see what's funny?

LEO Not really.

NATHAN Ah well, you're an Englishman. Leonard Chamberlain!

Nathan seems to find that mordantly funny.
Rosa extracts cakes from the Demel box.

ROSA The first time I came back after the war—January '46—I was so excited to see that Demel was still there I went in and ordered coffee and cake. The waiter said, 'We have no coffee and no cakes.' 'Oh. What have you got, then?' 'Camomile tea.' So I had camomile tea. We can go to Demel after the Belvedere to see Aunt Gretl's portrait. And there's the Bruegels in the Kunsthistorisches Museum, you should see them. What would *you* like to see in Vienna, Leo?

LEO I don't know. I'll have to come back for longer.

ROSA Do you like opera? We have opera. It's a shame you're just too soon for the new Opera House. It was supposed to be ready in time for the signing of the State Treaty so that the politicians and bigwigs could celebrate with Beethoven, including hundreds of de-nazified Nazis. Not to mention the ones in the orchestra. But never mind. After ten years of Allied occupation Austria is a sovereign nation. The crowd cheering outside the Belvedere Palace was smaller than the one which greeted Hitler but it was raining.

LEO Did the old Opera House burn down?

ROSA No, it was bombed by the Americans. When the fighting reached Italy, it brought Vienna in range. The Merz factory was flattened too. No more family business.

NATHAN And not much family. A New Yorker, an Austrian, and a clean young Englishman. By the way, Leo, what is it with Leonard? Your name was Leopold. Too Jewish?

LEO (*good-humoured*) Go and boil your head, Nathan. I'm sorry you had a rotten war.

Nathan has a paroxysm of laughter.

NATHAN 'A rotten war'!

LEO (*holds his ground*) Yes. I'm sorry. I'm sorry about your mother and father and . . . I can just imagine . . .

Rosa flinches at the foolishness of it, and jumps to cut it off.

ROSA Just leave it, Leo.

NATHAN What can you imagine?

ROSA And you, too!

NATHAN You see, *it's all one subject*, the sieg-heiling mobs in the streets, and Jews made to run naked to the gas with the guards shouting at them, the *dogs* shouting at them, shit running down their legs—

ROSA We've all read about it, Nathan!
(*To Leo.*) Haven't you?

Leo nods.

LEO What have I done wrong?

NATHAN Nothing. You're an accident of history.

LEO The Germans killed my mother, too—in the Blitz.

NATHAN Oh, in the Blitz! I can just imagine! But let's not get into a competition about whose mother—

ROSA Nathan! Stop being a schmuck.

NATHAN (*ignoring*) The Germans didn't kill your father, though.

LEO No. He's married again, still going strong.

NATHAN Your father, Leonard. It was the Austrians who killed your father.

LEO Oh. Yes.

NATHAN Before the war. 1934.

LEO I know.

NATHAN I remember it. We were sent home from school when the lights went out. It was winter, so the days got dark early. General strike! We were excited. A machine gun post on the corner! In the Old City, the streets were completely deserted. All the shops had their shutters down. My mother lit candles, and we waited. Then—boom! Artillery fire! Would you believe it? A showdown! The army was shelling the Karl-Marx flats, the pride of Red Vienna! Proper Austria, Catholic, baroque Austria in *Merry Widow* uniforms and white stockings was going to teach those rioters with their armed wing of socialists and Jews a lesson! Boom, boom! Hundreds dead, including your father, Aaron Rosenbaum. I honour him. You changed your name.

LEO My mother didn't want me to go to school with a German name. I was Leonard Chamberlain from when I was eight. She never talked about home and family. She didn't want me to have Jewish relatives in case Hitler won. She wanted me to be an English boy. I didn't mind. I was pleased. At school we were fighting the war through comic books where all the Germans were Nazis yelling in terror as our fighter pilots and commandos blew them to kingdom come. We were top country! I loved being English . . . English books, and the seaside and listening to the radio . . . Mother and I only spoke English. I didn't know I had an accent till I lost it. Mummy never lost hers. When she was killed . . . (*He tails off.*) No, I think that's enough of that.

Pause.

For Percy, to be stoical was to show character. You took the blow and carried on. He came home from the Ministry of Information, I came home from boarding school, we buried my mother, then we carried on.

Pause.

I turned out to be good at cricket . . . ended up getting my Blue.

NATHAN I don't think he's Jewish.
Do you remember this room?

Leo looks about him.

LEO I didn't live here, did I?

NATHAN For a few weeks before you left for England with Nellie and Percy. Until you were four you lived in the Karl-Marx Hof. I can show you. You can still see the bullet marks. When the Federal government destroyed your home, Nellie took you to live with your Grandma Eva. After *Anschluss*, their building was Aryanised, and you all had to cram into here. But you don't remember anything!
Kannst du das glauben? [*Do you believe this?*]

ROSA Do I believe in suppressed memory? In *Austria*?

NATHAN So you don't remember how the mob made off with your Great-Aunt Gretl's portrait?

LEO No. I don't.

ROSA Nor do you, Nathan. I didn't want to mention it but you weren't here.

NATHAN What? I wasn't here?

ROSA You didn't live here until Sally and Zac were evicted.

NATHAN But I remember it!

ROSA I believe in *false* memory too. What you described did happen to people, but what happened with Gretl's portrait was different. Sally wrote to me in New York. A Brownshirt arrived here unannounced, with two Wehrmacht soldiers. They went from room to room making a list. Hermann signed for what they took. I got this place back with less, and I'm going to get Gretl back.

She points at the wall.

I'm going to hang her right there.

NATHAN They'll drag it out for years. They'll tell you to apply to Bonn. (*To Leo.*) Gretl's portrait is in legal no-man's-land. If it's to be given back, it's not enough to know where it is. It's necessary to know who's got it to *give* back.

LEO Does it make any difference, morally?

NATHAN Morality makes no difference legally. Was Austria a defeated enemy, annexed to the Third Reich? Or was she an occupied country, Hitler's first victim? Under the law as it stood, when Hermann threw himself down the stairwell of the tenement in Leopoldstadt, was he still the owner of the portrait? Did the title pass to Jacob—?

LEO Jesus. Did Hermann kill himself?

ROSA *Hundreds* of Jews killed themselves after *Anschluss*—mostly middle-class Jews. Didn't you know that?

LEO And Jacob too?

ROSA No. Jacob killed himself when the war was over.

LEO When it was *over*? Why?

Nathan and Rosa are incapacitated by the question.

ROSA (*sharply*) You haven't earned the right . . . in your fool's ignorance—

NATHAN Come on, he's a kid.

ROSA He's only six years younger than you!

NATHAN (*wearily*) Yes, but what six.

LEO Hang on. I didn't know you existed till yesterday.

ROSA That's not an excuse, Leo! You knew you were Jewish.

LEO When? Yes, obviously I *knew*. But you don't understand. In England it wasn't something you had to *know*, or something people had to know about other people. I can't remember anyone asking me. It was the Book of Common Prayer if you could be bothered, and a carol service at Christmas.

ROSA It's not about where you worship.

LEO No. I can see that. I suppose if I'd wanted to join some snobby golf club . . .

ROSA That's not snobbery. It's anti-Semitism.

LEO Well, I take your point. But being made British was the greatest good fortune that could possibly have happened to me.

NATHAN Top country.

The merest suspicion of a sneer stings Leo into a retaliation.

LEO Well, we stood alone—didn't we!

NATHAN Whooh!

LEO And *ooh* to you too! Until Hitler turned on Russia, it was just us. I'm proud to be British, to belong to a nation which is looked up to for . . . you know . . . fair play and parliament and freedom of everything, asylum for exiles and refugees, the Royal Navy, the royal family . . . You're making me self-conscious now. But that's the way I've been left facing. Oh, I forgot Shakespeare.

I was quite pleased to have Jewish blood. To my mind it's a little bit of a distinction, a . . . an exotic fact from my life gone by. I knew I'd had a narrow squeak thanks to Percy . . . really, a charmed life, when you thought about it.

Rosa stands up with a jerk. She has to leave the room. Nathan is completely alert to her.

NATHAN So he was on a different train. What about it?

Rosa ignores him and leaves.

LEO I didn't mean to upset her.

NATHAN The funny thing is, you're more Jewish than we are. My Grandma Wilma married out, so Rosa and Sally had only two Jewish grandparents. The Nazis called them *mischlinge*. Half-breeds. Half-Jews. More than enough by the Nuremberg Laws. I'm three-quarters Jewish. But you're the whole catastrophe. Have some more cake.

LEO All right. Did many Jews come back like you?

NATHAN Not so many. But some. There were a few thousand who never left, living below the surface with a gentile husband or wife. U-boats, they were called. We're not enough to count politically. There are far more votes in leftover Nazis, half a million of them maybe, and no party wants to antagonise a bloc like that. Helping the interests of the Jews is not a vote-winner. We were more welcome under the Emperor.

LEO Why did you come back?

NATHAN Who the hell are they to tell me I'm not wanted?
We were ten per cent of the Viennese and fifty per cent of the
university graduates, of lawyers, doctors, writers, philosophers,
artists, architects, composers . . . Without the Jews Vienna was
mothballed like a carnival costume. There was that, and there's the
horse chestnut trees in the Hauptallee. This is my town.

LEO Yes, I see.

NATHAN I was in a DP camp in the American sector for a year.
Displaced Persons. But America had a DP quota. Everywhere had
a DP quota, and Palestine wasn't taking Jews because the British
had a deal with the Arabs. By the time the British made Palestine
the UN's problem, and the UN created the land of Israel, I was
in New York, twenty-four years old and in a math class at City
College. My charmed life. I came back in 1949. Orson Welles was
up on the Big Wheel. Theodor Herzl's coffin was being dug up for
reburial in Jerusalem.

LEO Are you back for good?

NATHAN Who can say? Austria is officially innocent. The ecstatic
multitudes who welcomed Hitler—innocent victims. Half the
camp guards were Austrians—innocent victims. The State Treaty
suits everybody. Austria is now in the front line of the Cold War.
So American dollars have kept us afloat. Demel has coffee and
cakes again. *Fidelio* will be the first performance in the new Opera
House, conducted by an ex-Nazi. Anti-Semitism is a political fact.
It's a bit soon for it to be a party platform, but when it is, there'll be
Austrians to vote for it.

LEO It can't happen again, Nathan!

NATHAN I bow to your experience. I'm sorry—Aunt Rosa told
me what you do in England but I've forgotten.

LEO I don't do anything much. I write funny books. I've written
two. Short but funny. Or not funny but short. They caught on

anyway. And I speak. After dinner, ten guineas a pop. But in Vienna it was a panel of British humorists, courtesy of the British Council.

NATHAN Yes, Aunt Rosa read an announcement in *Die Presse*.

LEO That's right. I think it went rather well.

NATHAN She phoned me afterwards—'I've found Cousin Nellie's boy!'

Leo comes over to offer a slice of cake on a plate.

Yes, she's upset.

No one is born eight years old. Leonard Chamberlain's life is Leo Rosenbaum's life continued. His family is your family. But you live as if without history, as if you throw no shadow behind you. You wanted to know why Jacob killed himself. It was because he didn't think he deserved to be saved when so many died.

He ignores the plate but examines Leo's hand, gently spreading the flesh between finger and thumb.

Do you know why you've got a scar there? You cut yourself on a broken cup. Your Great-Uncle Ernst, Aunt Rosa's dad, my grandad, sweet Ernst, the doctor in the family, sewed it up. (*Pause.*) Do you remember that?

Longer pause.
Leo nods.

(*Gently.*) I don't want any cake.

Leo goes and puts the plate back. He sits down.

It's okay, Leo.

Leo starts to cry silently. Nathan waits.

Do you remember about the broken cup?

Leo nods.

That was the last day you were in this room.

Leo nods. He says something.

What?

LEO   Cat's cradle.

NATHAN (*delighted*)   Cat's cradle! Do you remember me?

Leo shakes his head.

It was your grandpa showing us. I'm still playing cat's cradle, only I call it dynamical systems. I loved your Grandpa Ludwig. He lost his wits somewhat, but he showed me mathematics till they took him away two years after. He was desperate because he thought he'd found a new way into the Riemann Hypothesis but only in his head, and by that time nobody had a pencil.

Rosa enters briskly with a large A3 sheet of paper, on which she has drawn the family tree. She gives it to Leo.

ROSA   I wrote down the family tree for you to take home.

LEO   Thank you.

She notes an alteration in Leo, and raises an eyebrow at Nathan.

NATHAN   We've been exchanging memories.

ROSA   Ah. So what's the first thing you can remember, Leo?

LEO   I'm very sorry, Aunt Rosa.

ROSA   I have worse things to say sorry for. I'm very sorry, Nathan.

NATHAN   Don't mention it.

ROSA (*to Leo*)   There was a meeting of lots of countries, on Lake Geneva. The refugees problem. America explained there was a quota for Austrian Jews, and it couldn't be exceeded. My lawyer said: the quota is reducing every day—just do Sally and Zac and the kids—don't give them a reason for parking your application— you can come back for your dad, your aunties, cousins . . . And

I said no. Everybody. I agree to be financially responsible for everybody. Me on eighty-five dollars a month. But I got them. The visas came through the day Germany invaded Poland, and the Nazis closed the frontiers. After that, not a single Jew left Austria except in a cattle car.

But it turned out America never filled the quota. It let in ten thousand fewer Jewish refugees than the quota.

Nathan barks a laugh.

NATHAN   If you don't think that's funny, you're not close enough.

But his laughter is overtaken by his agony. He starts to howl.
Leo doesn't know how to respond.
Rosa, smoking, watches Nathan dispassionately.

ROSA   Right. I'm a Viennese Freudian analyst in New York with an office on the Upper East Side, I should complain?
(*To Leo, brightly.*) The first thing I can remember is the most shameful thing that ever happened to me, the absolute worst thing. I forgot where I'd hidden the afikomen.

Leo doesn't understand.

1900.
Little Rosa, on the instant, runs across, bawling in shame, and a beat later the room is inundated by the Seder party, amused and consternated, searching everywhere for the piece of matzo which Rosa has hidden.
Hermann, Ludwig and Ernst have opted out with an unceremonious glass of wine.
Sally grabs hold of Rosa, to stop her running out.

SALLY   Think!

Rosa bawls.

LUDWIG   L'Chaim.

HERMANN   Mazel tov.

ERNST   Cheers.

The rest of the family are all searching while Rosa bawls.
Gretl, nominally in the search party, has a plan of her own.

SEARCH PARTY . . . Did anybody see which way she went?—I
bet it's in the cigar box—(*Sally.*) What are we going to do?
What are we going to do?—(*Pauli.*) Don't cry, Rosa!—Look
in the cupboard—Try the bookcase—(*Jacob.*) Is it in the room
somewhere, Rosa?—(*Emilia, to Rosa.*) Did you eat it? You can tell
Grandma.

And suchlike, until Gretl shouts over the noise. She holds up the matzo.

GRETL Here it is!

General rejoicing. Rosa stops bawling.

SEARCH PARTY Hurrah—Well done, Gretl!—Where was it?—
Sit down everyone!—Where did she hide it?—Do you remember
now?

Hermann isn't fooled.

HERMANN (*to Gretl only*) Another miracle.

GRETL Oh, Hermann! I love the Seder! Why didn't you tell me?
It's a dinner party!

PAULI It just goes to show what a clever place you found, Rosa.

*Hanna needs a break. As the Seder meal reconvenes, she sits at the
piano and finds the missing matzo under the lid.*
She is amused. She tosses the matzo aside and starts to play quietly.

GRETL Hanna! Play a waltz! (*To Hermann.*) Can we dance?

WILMA It's a Seder, Gretl, not a knees-up.

HERMANN Later.

The clock hasn't stopped for Rosa, Nathan and Leo.
Leo is looking at the family tree.

ROSA Emilia died in her own bed.

LEO Hermann, suicide.

ROSA Passover, 1939.

LEO Gretl?

ROSA Brain tumour. December 1938.

LEO Jacob.

ROSA Suicide, 1946.

LEO Eva.

ROSA She died on the transport, 1943.

LEO Ludwig.

ROSA Steinhof, 1941.

LEO Pauli.

ROSA Verdun, 1916.

LEO Nellie. The Blitz.
Aaron. Artillery fire, Vienna.
Wilma.

ROSA (*correcting*) Vilma. She died.

LEO Ernst.

ROSA Auschwitz.

LEO Hanna.

ROSA Auschwitz.

LEO Kurt.

ROSA Dachau, 1938.

LEO Zacharia.

NATHAN Death march. Nowhere.

LEO Sally.

ROSA Auschwitz.

LEO Mimi.

ROSA Auschwitz.

LEO Bella.

ROSA Auschwitz.

LEO Hermine.

ROSA Auschwitz.

LEO Heini.

ROSA Auschwitz.

Pause.
Leo folds the paper.
Hanna continues to play as the three sit there as though listening.
The scene fades out.